Mary Hull

Columbus and what he found

Mary Hull

Columbus and what he found

ISBN/EAN: 9783743324305

Manufactured in Europe, USA, Canada, Australia, Japa

Cover: Foto ©ninafisch / pixelio.de

Manufactured and distributed by brebook publishing software (www.brebook.com)

Mary Hull

Columbus and what he found

COLUMBUS

AND

WHAT HE FOUND

BY
MARY H. HULL

✦✦✦

CHICAGO
Woman's Temperance Publishing Association
1892

To my own
Marion, Horace and Morton,
and their young friends,
Harold and Rush, John, Marion and Ida, Harold and
Margery, Harvey, Emeline, Edna and Rex,
I dedicate this book.
It owes very much to your eager
faces and questions,
as, with pencils and notebooks in hand,
you helped me to find
Columbus,
What He Found, and How He Found It.

PREFACE.

The immortal deed of Columbus will never lose its hold upon the heart of humanity, whatever the criticisms upon it. It will always be told, not only for what was found, but because simple heroism--the same element which has immortalized Greek heroic tales—will always move us, head and heart.

It is strange that, great and simple as Columbus was, we have made so little use of his story for the children, compared with that of other historic characters.

In the stilted past, for some reason, the head has made most of the estimates of the profits and losses to all concerned in this affair. We have not really known the man Columbus; hence we have not loved him. The deed has so blessed and dazzled us we have known only *it*.

The world is growing simpler and sincerer and more kind. The heart shall yet do its reckoning and shall find the humanity of it all. For during a time of slavish bondage to rules and rank, regulations and institutions, here was a man, in spite of them, perfectly true to himself and his God.

" The greatest miracle among ye is,
Here stands a man."

Mentally, morally and physically, a most manly man is Columbus—and only a man. Why may we not take his character and personality, together with his position in the world of geography and history, and make him a sublime figure; one which may well stand to personify, as it were, these two so-called "studies," for at least the intermediate world of childhood? This great intermediate world is at present most hungry for natural methods of instruction. As Washington with his "pony" and "hatchet" personifies patriotism in the Kindergarten world, why may not the characteristics of Columbus serve the youth of this yet young land, better than they have heretofore? So much real life-blood was the cost of this great deed, that there is an infinite amount of material for any parent or teacher who cares to quicken a live interest in that which is a living study, begetting life.

Not that hero-worship, unrestrained, is the object, but that something warmly human may stir the heart and mind through arresting the attention and securing an interest in human affairs. It is no fable. The wanderings and wonderings of this modern Ulysses are all so real that naught but heroism, self-denial to the point of self-discovery, can be breathed into the young American if it be simply, sincerely and sympathetically placed before him.

This is what I have tried to do in the present volume. The *motif* was born of interest in my own children, and it developed as I caught more of the thought of the Kindergartners through my acquaintance with the *Kindergarten Magazine* and its editor, Miss Andrea Hofer. I here wish to make acknowledgment of her most valuable suggestions, real aid, and encouragement in attempting such a work as this in these days of dire criticism and research. With original translations from the writings of Fernandez de Navarrette and Las Casas, whose great works are mines of wealth for all writers on Columbus in this century; with Irving and Lamartine, Arthur Helps, Mackie and others to sweeten and inspire one's spirit, and with Winsor to provoke it, and with the able American historian, John Fiske, at the very last to confirm the positions taken, I have only to say I have done my best and am greatly indebted to them all.

The World's Fair is at hand; the greatest panorama of the ages is to be presented to our young folks. Columbus has come to his earthly kingdom, and the children cannot too well know him, and through him what happened.

Columbus has come to stay, even after the World's Fair is over. We have, somehow, reached a vantage-ground whence we are able not only to conceive of this lonely, single-handed, manly man and his inherent genius and patience and faith, but we have also come to a point of National birth where we begin universally to appreciate ourselves as a Nation, and those who helped to create us. We are unifying more and more, and are a peculiar people. *America* will be stimulated in all her powers as never before, by all that shall be born of the Columbian Exposition. May the youth of America inherit their full birthright. M. H. H.

Columbus and What He Found.

I.

What is it? What was born four hundred years ago? Was it a child? Yes, that is what it was, and the largest and most beautiful one that ever was born.

This child seems almost to have come up out of the sea, as Venus did in the great stories of old, for that is where Columbus first found her, and it was in the very midst of the sea that she first came to life.

The child is America, often sweetly called Columbia; and this book is about how this child was born.

The Great Birthday. It is now just four hundred years since she was born, and I suppose you already know of the great birthday party we are going to have. The whole world is invited, and such a "time" as it will be, you have never seen and never will see again in a hundred years; so let us be wisely ready.

Nearly every country on the globe is either an uncle, a cousin, an aunt, or a grandmother or a grandfather, or a great-grandfather, to this young child, and we must know about them or we will not be very happy at the party. So the sooner we begin to learn of them the better for us.

This little birthday book, then, is an effort to introduce you to the real "Columbia, the Gem of the Ocean," and to tell you about her relatives, and to prepare you for the great birthday party,

The World's Fair.

II.

The very first thing, boys and girls, shall be to go and see the spot which yet lies under the sun, where a big-eyed hero boy began to live.

There has been a great deal of discussion as to where Columbus was born, but since the conclusions at the last are that it was Genoa, we will go there at once, for we have no use for talk here, and will only try to see what the boy saw, since it is Columbus himself we are most interested in.

The City of Genoa.

I invite you to the city of Genoa, to the city where Columbus began his wonderful life in 1435 or 1436, and where he combed wool and dreamed dreams, no doubt, of the great sea and its secrets.

Genoa is one of the most picturesque places

in the world, and very old, older than Rome. It was the greatest city in Europe, once. When Columbus was born, Genoa and Venice were capitals of two of the greatest powers in Europe.

Genoa was a dreamy, beautiful spot, but not a sleepy town; it was just the place in which an imaginative boy should be born.

Come with me and step into this little boat, and let us go out into the sea, off Genoa, and look back at it. At the very farthest faint line next to the sky, beyond the city, you will see the great Alpine mountains peeping over everything; and right on this side of them, do you trace the Apennines? And sloping on and on, down toward us, lie the hills right back of the town; all the green beauty of the hills, and plains, do you see it clustering there? And nearer, what is that around the city? That is a wall peeping out here and there. A wall so huge as that, is a thing which we in America never see. What can it be for? In Europe you nearly always find a wall about a city. Why? Because the world used to fight so much. Within the wall see the beautiful churches rise high above everything — and those broad palaces and promenades yonder, with the houses and gardens surrounding.

The city which we have just looked at is now about as big as our Milwaukee. And this is all I can stop to tell you about Genoa, but you can read in many books of old Genoa and the brave Genoese.

What kind of a boy was this who lived at Genoa? You must know how Columbus discovered himself, first, and found a great deal inside of his own mind long before he found the outside; that is, he thought for himself his own thoughts. The greatest discovery in earth or heaven is to find one's self.

The Boy.

This is the great lesson of the life of Columbus for our boys and girls to-day. Of course, when he was a little boy, and until he was a man, he did n't know exactly what that thing was which he should discover, but he knew there was something to be discovered. I believe every one of us not only may be, but should be, a born discoverer. Our main business in the world is to do this.

Discoveries.

For instance, if I were not to do any discovering for myself in this world, but just see things as you see them, why, then I would only need to look out into the world through your eyes. But I do not do that; I have a pair of eyes of my own. Some people always forget to look out of their own eyes, so they learn only old things—and it is not the boys and girls alone who forget.

The boy Columbus did both—he learned and he discovered. His mind ran free in thinking out his own thoughts while he was listening also to the thoughts of others.

He was a real boy, too, not only, as I imagine, making boats and such things for himself, but we know he helped his father, doing real work. His father had a business, and a very good one in those days. He was a wool-comber and some say he was a weaver, also. They worked together, and many a day, no doubt, they talked of all that was going on in the world, for there were wonderful stories to tell in those times.

There were three younger children in the family; two were brothers to Columbus, **The Family.** and their names were Diego and Bartholomew. There was a sister also. No doubt she was good, too, yet women in those days, unless they were queens or something great, did not figure greatly in the world's doings. So we never hear much about her, except that she married somebody.

The father's name was Dominico, and the mother's was Susanna Fontanarossa. And right here let me tell you Columbus' own name. He was really Christoforo Colombo, in the Italian language, and was not Columbus until he became a great admiral of the Ocean Sea. In Spanish his name was Christoval Colon, and while he lived in Spain he was thus called. He then Latinized it and made it Christopher Columbus, as was the custom of the time. So let us call him Colombo while we think of him a boy at home, for that is what his father and mother were called in the sweet Italian language.

The best business of all, thought this boy, must be the business of the sea:—and who would not think so, if it lay ever before our eyes so beautiful and inviting? His father seemed to understand him, for he let him study those studies which should best fit him for a life upon the water. Colombo first discovered this in himself, and his father was good enough to discover it in him also, and allow him to prepare for it. The boy and his father were real friends.

Colombo had distant relatives by his own name who were great water-men, and fond of doing brave, daring, even wicked deeds, and so our boy sailed with them early in life, when he was but fourteen years of age. We must now find out something about this sea business, and see what Colombo must have watched every day of his life, for you know by the map that Genoa is situated on the Mediterranean.

Venice is on the same sea, and you notice they are not very far apart from each other—only across Italy. But that little bit of land lying between them kept them farther apart than did all the distance by water down around the whole of Italy. You must remember that vessels were the main things in the world to go about in. It was a dreadful under-

The Sea.

taking to travel over ground, especially in a mountainous country; and you remember those mountain ranges that lie back of Genoa. It was always very hard, slow work to go anywhere except by water, until—just think!—only within the last forty or fifty years.

It is only within a few years that people could fly around on land, by steam. The poor old world, or, rather, everybody in it, for thousands of years had to go about either afoot, on horseback, or on camel-back, or be drawn by animals in chariots, carts or wagons, or in very poor, queer carriages. Not another way was there under the sun for people to travel around any easier or faster over mountains, or through mud. It took weeks and weeks to bury even a queen, four hundred years ago, in Colombo's time; for when the beautiful Queen Isabella died, we are told her subjects suffered greatly going up and down hills and through mud for miles, to attend the funeral.

Let me tell you something, right here. Less than fifty years ago, a gentleman living in Cincinnati was offered a fine position on a newspaper in Chicago, and he did not accept it because the journey of two weeks, by river, canal and lakes, from Cincinnati to Chicago, would be too hard for his family. Now, you can go to bed in a "sleeper" in either of these cities, and waken in the morning in the other city, having been tucked up warmly in a most comfortable bed all night.

It is no wonder, then, that boats, ships and the business of the water were great things in the world at that day, and no wonder that the boy Colombo longed for the sea. But even the sea vessels did not go by steam as they do now, only by sails and oars.

All around the Mediterranean is where the world began really to live and move for thousands of years before Colombo was born. Around this sea, not a hundredth part as big as the Atlantic (and your map will prove it), is where all the living, moving world for thousands of years had been crowded. And even there, they only lived on the edges of the land and never moved very far from the water.

The World around the Mediterranean.

The old Jews lived at the east end of the sea. You know the story of the long, slow journeys of Abraham, Isaac and Jacob, with their horses and camels, flocks and herds, over this eastern land, and of the children of Israel as they went from old Egypt to Palestine, the promised land.

Greece, on this wonderful sea, is also the spot where a great era passed in the history of the world. Years and years the people there carved wonderful sculpture and thought wonderful thoughts.

Then, here, in Italy (shaped like an old-fashioned boot), hanging down into this crowded little sea, centered the great Roman Empire with the Cæsars at its head.

Thick and fast, humanity had piled itself and its great history around this wonderful center. No, not "thick and fast,"—that is a mistake, for not fast did they come to live here. How long do you suppose history was in creeping from the time of Abraham, over here in Palestine, to the time of the Cæsars down here at Rome? Why, nearly two thousand years. And how long from this two thousand years when the Cæsars ruled Rome—that's about the time Jesus Christ was born over here in Palestine—do you suppose it is, until now? Why, you know that, it is one thousand eight hundred and ninety-two years! Just see how we talk about time, old Father Time.

Now all these years, except the last little four hundred years when Co-

Father Time. lumbus found another great sea to cross, moving humanity had crowded itself—not so "fast," but very "thick"—around this Mediterranean Sea. For how long? Shall we figure on that?

The 1892 years, with which we date all our letters and legal papers, make what we call our Christian era, the time from Christ until now (the sign is A. D.); add to it the two thousand years B. C. (before Christ), that is, go to the time of Abraham, and you have three thousand eight hundred and ninety-two years. Subtract these last important four hundred years and we have three thousand four hundred and ninety-two years still left. Just think how, for all this long time, people crowded around this sea before Columbus discovered a greater one!

Now wait, there was another very strange thing in the world always. No one yet knows how long there had been another lot of people over in what we now call China, India, Japan, etc., who were never-moving people. They did

Far East.

not know anything about the "world," and the "world" did n't know anything about them. They did not even know about each other when many miles apart. (By the word "world," we mean the thinking, moving world, that which is thinking and moving yet.)

These people around the sea were really "the world," for they found out things, while China has found out very little as yet, and had never heard of any world beyond her own save that there were people in the West called the Latins, until some one or two hundred years before Colombo was born! Then a wonderful man named Marco Polo found out all about this Far East. And this Far East king, called Kubla-Khan, found out from Marco Polo all about the Latins. "Latins" is the best name for our Mediterranean Sea people; for a few hundred years they were Grecians, then after that, when there were still more of them, they were Romans (and spoke Latin), so we will call them Latins for the present. We are going to the very bottom of this thing, to find out just what that child found out, for we can. Do you not believe we can?

Now Marco Polo climbed over to the Far East and back, somehow, and spent twenty-six years doing so, and then wrote a book which excited everybody the more and more they read it. It told most wonderful things about that region. Colombo's father must have heard of it, too, for the book was nearly two hundred years old when Colombo was born, and wealthy men of Genoa owned just such books.

Marco Polo.

Marco Polo was a Venetian, and he wrote the book while in prison at Genoa. He was there because the Genoese, once upon a time, overcame the Venetians in a fight, and he was taken prisoner with others. While there, for five or six years, with nothing else to do, he wrote up his travels. All books were written by hand, you know, until printing came. People did not believe half that was in this book, but Polo on his dying bed declared it was true, when he was questioned by his confessors. People have since found out that he wrote the truth. Columbus by his confessors. We know now that much of it was true. Columbus, in the main, believed every word of this book, of Cathay which Columbus expected to find in the Ocean Sea.

You must have a little of this book right here. You can get it for yourself, if you wish, and read of these most interesting travels.*

Marco Polo tells of many kingdoms and empires which he saw. He describes minutely and most quaintly very many strange things, and it helps us to understand how

---

*The Travels of Marco Polo, by Thos. W. Knox.

Columbus was always so sure he had found Marco Polo's "kingdoms" when he discovered our continent; for many strange things were very similar, such as climate, animals, birds, and, most of all, the mild temper of the inhabitants.

Marco Polo describes the great king of Cathay, his palace, his habits, and his capital city, Quinsay. It was like a story of fairyland. Read what Colombo read. No wonder he tried to find it:

"All the streets of the city are paved with stones or brick, so that you ride or travel in every direction without inconvenience. Were it not for this pavement you could not do so, for the country is very low and flat. But as the Great Khan's couriers could not gallop their horses over the pavement [the Great Khan was kinder to his horses than we in Chicago are], the side of the road is unpaved for their convenience. The pavement of the main street of the city, also, is laid out in two parallel ways of ten paces in width on either side, leaving a space in the middle laid with fine gravel, under which are vaulted drains that convey the rain-water into the canals; and thus the road is kept dry.

"You must know the city has three thousand baths, the water of which is supplied by springs; they are hot baths, and the people take great delight in frequenting them several times a month, for they are very cleanly in their persons. They are the largest and finest baths in the world; large enough for one hundred persons to bathe together."

The great Pacific, as we now know it to be, was called by Polo, "Ocean Sea," the same name by which the Mediterranean people had always called the Atlantic, so of course everybody thought there was but one ocean. "The Ocean Sea," wrote Marco Polo, "comes within twenty-five miles of the city, where there is a town and an excellent haven. A great river flows from the city of Quinsay to that sea haven, by which vessels can come to the city itself."

He tells how this Great Khan controlled nine great kingdoms, which had each a lesser king.

"In the whole of this vast country there are more than one thousand two hundred great and wealthy cities, without counting the towns and villages, which are in great numbers. And you may believe it for certain that in each of these one thousand two hundred cities the Great Khan has a garrison, and that the smallest five of such garrisons muster one thousand men each, while there are some of ten thousand, twenty thousand and thirty thousand, so that the total number of troops is something scarcely calculable.

"The people are idolaters, and since they were conquered by the Great Khan they use paper money. Both men and women are fair and comely, and for the most part clothe themselves in silk.

"The people have a custom that as soon as a child is born, they write down the day and hour, and the planet and sign under which its birth has taken place; so that every one among them knows the day of his birth. And when any one intends a journey [the greatest thing in the world was a journey], he goes to the astrologers and gives them particulars about his birth in order to learn whether he shall have good luck or no. These astrologers are very skillful in their business, and often their words come true, so the people have great faith in them.

"The natives of the city are men of peaceful character, both from education and from the example of their king, whose disposition is the same. They know nothing of handling arms, and keep none in their houses. In their dealings and in their manufactures they are thoroughly honest and truthful, and there is such a degree of good will and neighborly attachment among both men and women that you would take the people who live in the same street to be all of one family. You hear no feuds or noisy quarrels or discussions among them [surely they had no saloons].

"The city of Quinsay hath an hundred miles of compass [that is, a hundred miles around it]. And in it there are twelve thousand bridges of stone, so lofty that a great fleet could pass beneath them. And let no man marvel that there are so many bridges, for you see the whole city stands, as it were, in the water, and surrounded by water, so that a great many bridges are required to give free passage about it. And though the bridges are so high the approaches are so well contrived that horses and carts do cross them." This city is the modern Hangchau.

"Men of craft [men of business, that is],

they nor their wives ever touch a piece of work with their own hands, but live as nicely and delicately as if they were kings and queens. The wives, indeed, are most dainty and angelical creatures.

"Inside this city is a lake which has a compass of some thirty miles, and all around it are erected beautiful palaces and mansions, the most exquisite you can imagine; in the middle of the lake are two islands, on each of which stands a rich, beautiful and spacious edifice furnished in such style as to seem fit for the palace of an emperor. And when any one of the citizens desires to hold a marriage feast, or to give any other entertainment, it used to be done at one of these palaces; and everything would be found there ready to order, such as silver plate, trenchers, and dishes, napkins and table-cloths, and whatever else was needful. The king made this provision for the gratification of his people, and the place was open to every one who desired to give an entertainment. Sometimes there would be at these places an hundred different parties; some holding a banquet, others celebrating a wedding; and yet all would find good accommodations in the different apartments and pavilions, and that in so well-ordered a manner that one party was never in the way of another."

Just think of one hundred parties at one time! It is no wonder they called it "The City of Heaven," for that was their idea of heaven. Polo goes on giving descriptions of hospitals and "guards" (like our policemen), postmen and timekeepers, and many such things, so that it is not strange that he stops sometimes and says, "It seems past belief to one who merely hears it told, but I will write it down for you."

He tells about one thing that I cannot leave out, and that is how they gave the alarm for fire or danger of any kind.

"Within this city there is an eminence on which stands a tower, at the top of the tower is hung a slab of wood. Whenever fire or any other alarm breaks out in the city, a man who stands there with a mallet in his hand beats upon the slab, making a noise that is heard at a great distance." Was n't that a strange fire-bell?

Now hear a little about the king's palace:
"You must know a little of its demesne [its grounds] hath a compass of ten miles, all inclosed with lofty walls, and inside the walls are the finest and most delectable gardens upon earth. There are numerous fountains in it, also, and lakes full of fish. In the middle is the palace itself. It contains twenty great and handsome halls, one of which is more than the rest and affords room for a vast multitude to dine in. It is all painted in gold with representations of histories and birds and beasts, knights and dames, and many marvelous things. It forms really a

magnificent spectacle, for on all the walls and all the ceilings, you see nothing but paintings in gold. And besides these halls the palace contains one thousand large and handsome chambers all painted in gold and divers colors.

"From the Ocean Sea also come daily supplies of fish in great quantity. One would suppose so great a quantity could never be sold, and yet in a few hours the whole is cleared away. .... For a Venice groat of silver you can have a couple of geese and two couple of ducks. Then there are calves, beeves, kids and lambs, the flesh of which is eaten by the rich and the dignitaries. Indeed, they eat fish and flesh at the same meal.

"These markets make a dainty display of every kind of vegetables and fruits; there are pears of enormous size, weighing as much as ten pounds apiece, the pulp of which is white and fragrant like a confection, besides peaches in their season, both yellow and white, of every delicate flavor.

"These natives do not care much for wine, being used to that kind of their own made from rice and spices. To give you an example of the vast consumption in this city, let us take the article of *pepper* [his own italics], and that will enable you to estimate what must be the quantity of victuals provided for the general consumption. Now Messer Marco [he always says *Messer Marco* in speaking of himself, instead of saying *I*] heard it stated by one of the Great Khan's officers of customs, that the quantity of pepper introduced daily into the city of Quinsay amounted to forty-three loads, each load being equal to two hundred and twenty-three pounds." Imagine a city that used nine thousand five hundred and eighty-nine pounds of pepper in one day!

That is enough from the great Polo book. I imagine it is the book our Colombo boy in the frontispiece has been reading, as he sits so dreamily on the very outpost of some wharf—for see, his foot rests on the great ring to which vessels are fastened. Here he reads of a vast kingdom somewhere in the world where there are lakes of pearls, mountains of gold and beautiful stones; reads of that other magic king, "Prester John," reads of the "Roof of the World," where all suppose the garden of Paradise to be; and he reads of how they were idolaters, how they knew nothing of the Christian religion: and "O! what a world this is," he thinks, as he looks into the sea. "I love it, and I must discover all I can of it."

Late students and critics believe that Marco Polo's book led to the discovery of the New World more than any other one thing, for from Columbus' own writings he seems to have known every line of it, and was always inspired and led on to his discoveries by it.

III.

Colombo returned to his home from school in Pavia at fourteen years of age. Nobody seems to know how long he was there, or whether he had any more "school" of that kind or not. One thing we know, he had plenty of life-school, which was no doubt a better education for a great discoverer than a book-school could have been. His son—his first biographer—does not tell us any small things of his father's boyhood life, but only that he went to school at Pavia. That sounded great and really was great in those days, for school was not very easy to go to. It cost much money. There were but few schools in the world at that time. One at Pavia up in Italy among the mountains and one at Paris, France, were the two most important ones.

And what strange schools they were, without any books! Eyes and ears and hands had to be used instead; ears to hear what was told by teachers during lectures, and then eyes and hands to write the things down. In this way pupils had to be ready for examinations. Examination was recitation and recitation was examination all the time.

Colombo studied geography, astronomy and navigation, and some Latin. These **Colombo's Studies.** are pretty broad studies for a boy of fourteen, but they proved to be the great foundation of his life. His geography, indeed, must have been a puzzling and exciting study. It must have been based on Ptolemy's geography, which was then over one thousand three hundred years old. The Roman Empire, as it had been spread about the Mediterranean Sea, was correctly mapped out, but Africa was a queer-looking affair stretching out away to the south and to the west. Nobody knew how far it should go, for nobody had ever seen any farther south than what was then called Cape Nun, meaning none, nothing beyond. It is now called Cape Verde. You can see in your geography that it does appear to be the jumping-off place, with nothing beyond, and when we realize how very warm it is there so near the equator, we need not be surprised that the people thought it was boiling hot farther on, and probably was the edge of the world. So Cape Nun was a good name.

A queer-shaped England was in this geography; Iceland, called Ultima Thule, the end, was in a very strange place; so were Scotland and Ireland.

It decided that the ocean did not go to the end of the world, wherever that was, or however that was, as others had taught, but that land must be the end, or edge, for what would hold the water together if it were not surrounded by land? So all unknown land was termed Terra Incognita; that is, Land Unknown.

As to the shape of the earth, great uncertainty prevailed. Ptolemy lived at Alexandria, down on the southern coast of the Mediterranean Sea, in Egypt, to which nearly all the wonderful books of Greece and Rome were taken and where they were saved when the barbarians overran all Europe during what we call the Middle Ages of the world. He lived in the second century after Christ, and the geography had not been changed a great deal even when Colombo studied it in the fifteenth century, for so little had been found out in the world in all that time, which could change it.

The world, even this learning world around the Mediterranean, had not grown very fast, not to know more geography than Ptolemy did one thousand three hundred years before. Something happened to all Europe, and that is why it did n't learn faster in all those years. The next chapter will tell you what it was that happened.

Uncertainty as to the Shape of the Earth.
The Grecians and Romans away back before Christ, had some notion that the world was round, and Ptolemy dared to surmise something of the kind; he thought that it was shaped like half of a round apple cut through the middle, and resting on its flat side; for of course, said he, it had to stand on something.

We shall come to a time when Colombo, in his weary hunting, concluded it was more like a pear, with a sort of high part as a pear has at the stem end. He was pretty sure once that he had come to that part, and that it was the roof of the world, for Marco Polo had written about that roof. And as an earthly Paradise was the hope and dream of all the world through those Middle Ages, it seemed very likely to lie on the top of this pear-shaped world. Marco Polo described what he had seen on the "Roof of the World," and it was to him like Paradise, and so of course Columbus hoped he was near it when he seemed to come to a place where marvelous waters came pouring down as if from such a great roof. Poor man, he was only at the mouth of the Orinoco River. But this was during his fourth voyage, and I must not get so far ahead of my story.

This Paradise had been located in various places by old travelers, and was always an interesting place to hunt for. Once

Paradise.

it was supposed to be on the island of Ceylon in the Indian Ocean, but when that island came to be better known, the notion was given up and everybody supposed it was to be found in the wonderful land of Cathay. Marco Polo had surely found a strangely beautiful place, and since people supposed Paradise must be somewhere in the world, it is not surprising that Columbus put the thought of the Paradise, and the roof, and his idea of the pear-shaped world, all together, and supposed he was about to make this most interesting of all discoveries. Ponce de Leon, many years afterward, you know, also came to America fully expecting to find the Fountain of Youth.

To go back to our geography: Some ancients had said the world was round like a flat cake floating, instead of being round like an apple or a pear. Some had also come to the conclusion that it was in the form of a globe. But when Columbus was a boy, and a young man, people were talking about many wonderful new things, no matter what geographies taught.

The Portuguese had found out in 1412 that they could get past that Cape Nun and not be burned up. What a wonderful thing! They also discovered some new islands out in the Ocean

The Wild Stories Changed by the Portuguese.

Sea. Porto Santo was one, remember it. These things all meant wonderful possibilities. If one thing was done another could be done. The gates of the world seemed to be opening. The great doubts about water and land and the shape of the earth were going to be explained. Ignorance was growing to be unendurable to a few spirited souls. Good Prince Henry was one of the wisest. He founded a sort of school for navigation at Lisbon when Columbus was yet a boy at his home in Italy.

Yet others concluded that water was the end of the world instead of land, for the last thing seen by those who had sailed the farthest, was water, water everywhere. The world might end in a watery mist where it joined the sky, since the weather and water seemed to get hotter and hotter the farther toward the south one went. They knew that.

Wild stories were told about men getting into such hot places that they could n't get back again, and had been baked to death on their vessels. The hot sun over them and the hot water beneath, so roasted them that when one went to pick them up their arms came off their bodies. This was not all; people said there were boiling whirlpools away off there, which sucked the vessels right into hot water.

This awful south must have had a fearful look to little children when they were all alone at night, as they gazed off in that direction. Colombo, no doubt, heard these great sea stories when a boy; and, indeed, when he grew to be a man, even ready to sail into the great unknown, these stories had not improved any. They had been located farther away, however, as new discoveries were being made. Marco Polo did tell for truth, and I have read it in his book, how men would die and be baked in hot deserts.

You see, Colombo was studying a very queer sort of geography all his life; not book geography, for old Ptolemy was fast being changed by real geography. The Portuguese were moving about and making new and wonderful discoveries. These new discoveries required new maps, and this is what gave our Columbus a living when he came to be a man.

We must go back a little. Colombo commenced his sea-school, we say, at fourteen years of age, with men by the name of Colombo. Then he could go on studying astronomy, also, by watching the stars themselves; so his astronomy became actual as well as his geography. By sailing and "roughing it" for about ten years, until he was twenty-five years of age, he studied actual navigation by being in close contact with real water and waves and storms and calms, and learning to manage real vessels. All this, added to his studies at Pavia, made him a regular graduate of Divine Providence, because he early committed his way to God, and it would seem God took him and prepared him for his great work in life's school.

He sailed everywhere around the Mediterranean, and from this he passed out between those two great giant rocks on each side of the Strait of Gibraltar, into the mighty deep. How they must have seemed to his impressionable nature like great gods guarding the beautiful, homelike sea he had always known, from the great Ocean Sea. They always had to pass between them, and then his voyage would be up and down the coast, never very far from land. The Genoese were very brave men on water, and were often hired by other nations to do their fighting for them. This was probably the main business of the men with whom our young Colombo began his lessons in navigation. This was why he was sometimes supposed to be a pirate. We know merchants hired just such men to carry their goods to and fro from the Levant — the east end of the Mediterranean, to which precious silks and cloths came from the fabulous Far East.

Colombo in his ten years' life on the water learned, no doubt, about every kind of vessel.

Vessels of the Fifteenth Century.

I think you will like to know a little about what he learned; it will not take you more than ten minutes to get a pretty good idea.

There were merchant vessels (we have freight cars, instead) and war vessels of all sorts and sizes, though none could carry more than five hundred tons. The galleys were the most ancient of war vessels, and were used by the Egyptians, Greeks and Romans, hundreds of years before; sometimes they had many rows, or banks, of oars, one bank placed above the other. The top oars had to be the longest, so as to reach the water, and they would then be so heavy to handle that the end next to the "galley slave" who used it, had to be loaded with lead. Just think, the oar is the oldest and the youngest instrument used in navigation, and is the most like a human hand paddling along. The "galley slaves" were convicts and prisoners who would be chained to their places for years and years at a time, and there they would have to sit where they could see nothing while they worked these great oars, all working together by music or the sound of a bell.

When five rows of oars were used the vessel was called a quireme; when four rows, a quadreme; three rows, a trireme. In the fifteenth century, however, these galleys seldom had more than one row, or bank, of oars. These galleys were often very gorgeously adorned. They had a beak in front with which they would run against an enemy's vessel and break a hole in it. Now the use of gunpowder, you must know, made a wonderful change in the world, because it changed war methods. Men had fought with galleys of all sorts and shapes, but gunpowder made them of less and less use in war; yet up to the eighteenth century there still remained some sort of a galley.

The Maltese galley carried five hundred forty-nine persons, including the galley slaves. The gallea and galleon were the first improvements on the galley. The artillery was placed fore and aft, and had to shoot only in front or from behind, else they would kill their own oarsmen. In the gallea they relied on sails altogether and got rid of their oars, or had overhanging sides for oars. The galleon had the sides "tumble home," that is, bend in at the top so that sometimes the bottom of the boat was twice as wide as the top.

We read of our young Colombo having command of a galley, so you see he must have known about every little "nook and corner" in it.

There were also many other kinds of vessels, generally about three hundred tons weight. This was, perhaps, the weight of the largest of Columbus' three ships in which he first crossed the Atlantic. Nobody knows exactly—but from a reliable source we read his vessel was only sixty-three feet long,—twenty feet beam and fifty-one feet keel, the depth being ten and one-half feet. What a small vessel compared with the eight and ten thousand ton vessels, which are six hundred and eight hundred feet long, crossing the ocean nowadays!

Very few vessels had any decks in the fifteenth century. The forecastle was at first a sort of platform built out on the front of the ship for the archers and soldiers to stand on while they fought. Then these platforms came to be housed in, and then they were called forecastles. Inside this place, the ship's office business was transacted. Then vessels came to have a castle at each end of the boat. Finally these castles were made to cover the whole vessel; they were then "decked." There were also "topcastles" at the top of the masts where men would be stationed so that they could annoy the enemy with darts, missiles, stones, or anything of that kind. These were on the largest ships, and it took four or five years to build such an one.

Then there were other kinds. Carracks were next in size, and were more generally used in trade, mostly by the Genoese and Venetian, and were armed, for merchants in the Mediterranean Sea had to fight to keep from having their goods stolen from them. They were usually of one hundred to two hundred tons weight.

Barges and balingers were still smaller vessels with no "castles" on them. These were used for adventure and to reconnoitre, as they drew little water and could go in advance of larger vessels and find out how things were. When several of them went off on foreign voyages they usually sailed in "convoys," that is, a lot of them would sail together. Four barges and two balingers were capable of holding one hundred twenty men-at-arms and four hundred eighty archers and sailors.

Their fighting implements were habergeons, basinets (examine your dictionaries), bows and arrows, jacks, targets, lances and firing-barrels, fire-arrows and sometimes cannon.

The Armament of Ships.

In 1490 a Venetian historian writes of the "novelty of firearms" as follows, giving a pretty good description of our present gun. "The use of iron tubes," he says, "transmitted to us from Germany, is become important among our soldiery. These tubes by the force of fire, discharge leaden bullets with extraordinary violence, and wound from a distance. They are of the same shape and form as a cannon by which walls are battered, with this difference, however, that the latter are cast from brass, and are often of so great weight as to require iron and solid bound carriages, and a vast number of horses for their transportation. The tubes, on the other hand, are made of iron fixed on a wooden butt, so that one may be handled by every soldier singly. They are loaded by gunpowder which is easily kindled, and when the bullet has been rammed down they are discharged from the shoulder.

"The Council of Ten, anxious to obtain a supply of men skilled in these weapons, have collected from all quarters persons who are masters of their use, and have sent them into different towns to instruct the youth. Two adults from each village shall devote themselves to this every year. There shall be an assembly of these marksmen at some spot fixed by themselves for shooting at a target."

We thus see how people were interested in new things, and gunpowder was one of them.

Many vessels were highly ornamented. The sails were often gorgeous in color, and the front of the boat would be made into many interesting shapes, like that of a horse's head or a swan.

In the fifteenth century, for the first time, somebody thought of having a rudder made fast behind the vessel to be managed by ropes or chains, taking the place of two great oars which had formerly been used for steering the vessel.

The sails of the ship were a square one in front, called the mainsail, hung on a yard, the yard being fastened to the mainmast; the sails back of this were called lateen sails, were smaller and of a triangular shape, such as we have now, except that they were on crooked masts. The smaller boats had only lateen sails.

The compass was another new thing in those days. Marco Polo had found it in China and had brought it to Europe two hundred years before, but it was not in general use as a guide until many years after. At first it was called "sail-stone," "lodestone," "sailing-needle," etc., before it was developed into the "compass" that we know. But it was a most wonderful turning-point in navigation.

Colombo sailed in all sorts of ways, no doubt, for ten years, getting all sorts of lessons in navigation. He learned to be the greatest navigator the world has ever known, not only on wide, open, unknown seas, but also in strange and dangerous shallow waters, and among rocks and islands; not only in storm and peril, as you will see, but in times of peace. He never was "caught napping" but once, and then he ought to have napped if he had only had trusty sailors about him.

Toward the end of his schooling in navigation, when he was about twenty-five years old, we hear of him in a terrible wreck off the coast of Portugal. He may have been living in Portugal at the time, nobody knows for certain, but it seems he was certainly wrecked off the coast and remained in Portugal until he went to Spain. He certainly landed at this time in a very sorry plight near Lisbon.

His Wreck.

He was in command of a galley during a naval fight off the coast of Lisbon. His vessel grappled with the enemy's and both caught fire, his only escape being to jump into the water. He swam six miles to shore during a very high sea, with the help of an oar, and was much exhausted when he reached the end of his perilous journey. But he was a very strong and brave young man, and this was a time when muscle and courage saved him. But he landed, and with him landed the fate of our " Columbia, the gem of the ocean." Ah! if he had been lost then, there is no telling how much longer she would have remained unborn!

He was a long time ill from his terrible swim, but he recovered, and we next find him a regular attendant at church, and falling in love with a beautiful young lady.

IV.

"The term Middle Ages is applied to the period extending from 476 to the discovery of America in 1492."

History says this. Read it carefully: what Columbus did will always be talked about, because this discovery was the beginning of our Modern Age, and was the ending of the Middle Age.

That time called "Middle Ages" is what this talk is about, and I think it is the most interesting one we have, but you may "skip it" if you wish to hurry on after Columbus.

But since Columbus himself was made up out of this Middle Age, it is very important to know what the world was like and what our Colombo boy came to, and what he had to hear and see and study, or we cannot even imagine how it ever happened that he changed things so.

It is no wonder we are celebrating our four-hundredth birthday, by having a World's Fair. Learn all you can at this very time, for neither you nor any one now living will see another birthday like it.

Colombo changed things so, because he was born at just the right time, and because he believed he could do something. He saw that old geography did not know much, for it left things so unsettled about what the world was like.

He also said to himself that away back in the Ancient Ages (before the Middle Ages) Grecians and Romans knew more and better things than people do now. (Remember his "now" was in the fifteenth century.)

He believed, somehow, that those ancients were right about the world being like a pancake, floating on something, or perhaps that it was even a globe, although they only guessed at it. If they were right it must be proven. This great idea grew and grew with him.

No one knows exactly when it commenced.

For about one thousand years (from 476 to 1492) there had been so little learned about anything! Why?

The Middle Ages are also called Dark Ages. Why? Let us try and find out some of these "whys."

We will call the time of this "fall" one thousand years b. c., meaning by small b. c. *before Columbus;* I do not believe it is irreverent to call it so. You know what large B. C. means. For one thousand years b. c., it had been a strange, sad time with the whole world. The Roman Empire, the Cæsar's great Rome, fell all to pieces in 476 A. D., that is 476 years after Christ, who changed all dates.

Fall of the Roman Empire.

When it fell there seemed to be great darkness. All the beauty of art and learning and the refinement and civilization of the world were nearly destroyed; only ruins left! Many ruins of this time are now standing in the City of Rome.

The Roman Empire spread nearly all around the Mediterranean Sea; the city of Rome was the capital, the center of Roman power, so when we say Rome, we mean not only this city but the empire. Rome, the great, had now lost its hold, especially over its "West." The West then did not mean our West out here in the great, broad lands, but it meant the west end of the Mediterranean Sea. Spain used to be called Hispania, a word meaning "the outer edge." Spain was thought to be the west edge of the world, because people had no idea how big the world was. So West, b. c., was the western end of the Mediterranean Sea, and on up along France, and the British Isles.

Although this great Roman power had ruled nearly everything, even Palestine, Jesus' own country, yet it fell. It had the greatest and best laws the world had yet seen, except those of Moses, and they had governed only the little country of Palestine, and had been written 1500 years B. C. The Romans were the first people to build roads. They built great stone theaters, too. One was the Coliseum, whose ruins still stand; I fancy you have seen pictures of it. They built great buildings for holding their meetings, great porches, great arches, gateways with writings cut in them telling of great battles, and there they are standing yet, but Rome herself fell.

She fell because she grew so rich and ripe! She fell because she could no longer with her riches bless the world. God seems to have a way of letting things go to pieces if they do not do this. Rome could not bless the world any more, because as her people grew richer they became very vain and good-for-nothing. Heroism died out after the Cæsars, and the first thing the great power knew, there came a lot of

Why Did Rome Fall?

brave, ignorant, wild people, barbarians, who ruined all her finery.

Nobody can tell exactly where all these hordes of people came from. They are always called "The barbarians." They came from the north somewhere, and, anxious for fine things, they took possession of all they liked. What they did not like they utterly destroyed. So a condition of hopelessness fell over everything and the world's "Dark Ages" came on.

The Barbarians.

The barbarians were not quite like our wild Indians, yet they were not unlike them. In your school readers and histories you will read about them, for it was a wonderful one thousand years in which they ruled, and the world will always talk about them. These people were not all alike. They were in tribes, in droves. Some were called Huns, some were Teutons, some were Goths, Vandals, and so on. I cannot stop to tell you much about them, only to say that they were brave and ignorant and had none of the weaknesses of civilization.

There were thousand and thousands of these barbarians and they kept coming in droves for hundreds of years.

Rome, you see, was cultivated and beautiful but the people had grown lazy and weak. These fresh, free hordes of men who loved lawless liberty, were strong. They had liberty, but no law or order, hence they never had learned anything. The Romans had law but no liberty, and they were weak though they had learned much.

Do you see here are two great things coming right up against each other—Law and Liberty? These two things had to learn to live together: and the world grew dark while this was being learned. The hordes were accustomed to rule themselves. They knew nothing about kings and emperors and laws. Rome could not stand before them and she lost control of things; and all this happened in the fifth century—one thousand years b. c.

A strange kind of government just then made itself up out of the civilized ideas of Rome and the wild, free notions of the barbarians. It is called Feudal government. "Feud" means the right to a piece of land. Instead of the king or some ruler owning all the country, each man had the right to a piece of land. He paid a fee for this right, so that each feud meant something like fee. Then each man who was the head of a family could own his own land. After awhile, a man would have to fight some other man to keep him off that land (for he could n't put the land into his pocket) so feud came really to mean fight.

Feudal Government.

We cannot stop to find out all about feudalism, of course, but it is interesting to know about, since it was the time of knight errantry, chivalry and ever so many interesting things. The most important feature of

COLUMBUS AND WHAT HE FOUND. 67

feudalism was its idea of a freehold on land.

About the year 800 A. D., things began to settle down somewhat after those dreadful fightings and wars. The free men began to get rich. Families grew powerful, some more so than others, but they did not learn anything until the time when there came an emperor by the name of Char-

Charlemagne.

lemagne, who in 800 A. D. (600 b. c.) began to build schools and start the world to doing something besides eating and drinking.

The people had no thought, no books, no morals, but just dug in the ground and played and fought. They robbed each other as any other animals would: but the great thing that was coming into the world was a sort of freedom.

This was eight hundred years after Christ came into the world and His truth was only beginning to be felt as a power. Charlemagne had a dim notion that the people should be learning something. The school at Pavia, which Columbus attended six hundred years after, was one that he founded. His numerous daughters made copies from the old classical writings and people began to change again from barbarism to civilization. Charlemagne himself was so fond of study that he used to study while he ate his dinner, after he was a grown man and an emperor.

The old classical learning thus crept back into life. It had nearly been destroyed, you see, save that which was stored in monasteries or hustled off to Alexandria. Christianity, also, began to creep into those dark Middle Ages in Charlemagne's time. Greek and Roman learning came back but their pagan religion did not.

Just think what a poor, strange notion the
The Church. people had about this new kind of religion for a long, long time. There had been great religions in the

world before. The Romans and Greeks had imaginary gods sitting around on top of high mountains and in the sky, who ruled like mighty kings over all their wars, their seas, their agriculture. But they had no thought that any God ruled by love alone.

They thought gods must, of course, rule by power. And it is no wonder that when the new religion came into the world during these dark times, people supposed somehow it was to be a religion of power or it was of little good, so the Christian church strove to be a power, and it was.

The first real Christians like Peter and John and Paul, Justin Martyr, Tertullian, Origen, Chrysostom, Athanasius, Augustine—big names, but never mind—did not suppose Christianity to be a thing of pompous power, but later Christians did. The early Christians were great in being gentle, not powerful.

But old gods, to be good for anything had

to be powerful, so, of course, it was human to try to have Christianity a great power. And do you know people were forced into being Christians! When a great king came to be a Christian then he made all his people profess to be Christians.

So the Church of the lowly, loving Jesus came to be the greatest power on earth. It even made kings kneel down to the Popes. The Pope represented God on the earth. God, of course, owned the earth, they said, for He made it; then if the Pope was God's representative he must be the one who owned the land really, instead of anybody else, and people came to pay the Pope the fees for land. Columbus' most important permission to discover new land came from the Pope.

The Church grew to be so powerful that by the time Columbus was born all Europe belonged to it.

All this time of the Dark Ages, then, the

"Light of the World" was coming in, and although Christians at first made this mistake of honestly trying to rule the world as they thought God would rule it, by power, yet it was better Light than any before, for there was much love in it. Pagan religion had had none at all.

People were ready to die or to do anything for this Christ whom they loved, and oh! how they rejoiced when they heard He was coming to the earth again. The people had no Bibles to read, so they believed only what the priests told them. It is no wonder, then, that the priests got up some very queer things, so as to make the people obey them. They would read the Scriptures to them. They taught the people that Christ was coming back to the earth again when one thousand years from the time he first came had gone by, so in this tenth century, 1000 A. D., they began to look for Him.

The Crusaders.

Peter the Hermit preached everywhere telling this, and, filled with delight, millions and millions of these people we have been talking about, commenced climbing over the mountains and wading the rivers, going to Jerusalem, down at the east end of the precious sea, to meet Him. Peter said Jerusalem was where Jesus was crucified and it was where He would come again. So men, women and children, for two hundred years kept going to and from Jerusalem to see Jesus.

We are talking about centuries of time and millions of people: remember how great this all is. It will help you in all your studies of history and geography hereafter.

Now this going to and fro for so many years from Spain, France, England, Italy, and other countries, to Jerusalem, made a great change in Europe. Why? It was not because they found Christ at Jerusalem, for they were disappointed in that; it was not because they got into so many fights as they did when they got there, and found the Saracens had possession of Jerusalem (remember this, for Columbus tried to do something about it); but it made wonderful changes in Europe because it started the people moving around and finding out things about others besides themselves. So you see what there was left of civilization, what there was of learning and goodness, commenced again to grow when people moved about and thought.

Now all this was called "Crusading," and it was what made Genoa and Venice grow so fast in the tenth and eleventh centuries. People got very tired of going by land, so they went by water, instead. Genoa and Venice lay at the heads of two points of water not very far apart from each other, where travelers could take a vessel. Therefore great rivalry sprang up between these two powers. Each worked hard to get the most custom and become great in navigation.

People began to carry goods with them, and to trade them off for something else; they made money faster than by digging in the land. This was the beginning of real commerce.

Ah! Now you see things are ripening.

Jesus did not come to Jerusalem, but His spirit did come to all Europe through this. He made people know each other, and sometimes love each other. The new was really commencing, the world was beginning to move on.

In this tenth century the schools grew, the church grew, science grew, art grew, and commerce grew. This made a great change, but remember the change came slowly.

Marco Polo brought the compass, you know, in the twelfth century, and this brought many new ideas into navigation, for sailors could now guide their vessels at all times and need not wait for the sun to come out in the daytime or for the moon and stars at night.

I have told you how gunpowder made a great change in naval war, in vessels and in many ways. The greatest **Printing.** change of all, however, next to Columbus' discovery, was the thing which John Gutenburg found out, that writing could be done with something besides a man's hand. All books were written by hand, and always had been, up to the time that Columbus was born.

It was in Germany that men first found that a sort of impression, or imprint, could be taken of a lot of wooden letters all at one time, if they had ink on them. Then they found that a lot of these imprints could be made from one surface. And, oh, what a discovery! What secrets John Gutenburg kept to himself! He first used wooden letters tied together with strings. It was afterwards found that movable metal letters were more convenient.

The Bible was the first book that was printed. A man bought a beautiful copy, supposing it had been written by hand. Of course it cost a great deal of money, for such a book was the work of one man's lifetime. The owner was very proud of it, for it was so beautifully written. He showed it to another man and, behold, he had one just exactly like it! These surprises happening, set men to wondering how in the world this beautiful, even, clean writing could be done. The type imitated writing in Latin and the pages had beautiful colored pictures on them made by hand, and it was a marvel.

Do you know there is an original Gutenburg Bible in Chicago? It is the loan of Mr. Ellsworth to the Chicago Art Institute, and there it lies in a glass case for all to see. It is in two volumes; one lies shut and one lies open so people may see the outside and the inside without touching the precious relic. Mr. Ellsworth and his friend, Rev. Mr. Gunsaulus, in 1891, heard of this Bible being for sale, so they went to New York quite determined to buy it for Chicago, and they did, paying $14,000. There is but one other copy in the world. See it if you can, for it is a great prize.

Printing commenced secretly in Germany in 1436, and in 1462 it was made known. In 1465 printing was done at Paris, Milan, Venice and at Rome; it did not reach England until 1474. But just think how slowly it grew, after all, for even in 1492, the same year that Columbus discovered America, there were only sixty printed books in the world, that is, sixty different books. Forty-four of these books were in England. In 1500 it is said there were five hundred printing presses in all Europe, but they were clumsy things compared with what we have now.

The first printing press in our New World came to Mexico in 1536. Fifty years after, one was set up at Lima, South America; then over fifty years more passed by before one was set up at Cambridge, Massachusetts, in 1639.

The first printing press in our West was at Cincinnati in 1793, the next at St. Louis in 1808.

So, you see, printing was really a new way of getting along, and you can easily see what a wonderful discovery it was, for it lets thought and news run through a very wide and rapid channel from one end of the earth to the other. Before printing came, all thought was crowded into very few libraries, and it generally stayed there.

Before Columbus discovered America and while people lived only along sea-coasts, the world was crowded for room; Columbus was just needed. A man of God, he was inspired to find new ground. This land around the sea had been trodden on so many years, and had so many old things tumbling down on it that the world needed a new continent. Columbus did not know all that, he just did his own work, and did greater things than he knew.

Now these Middle Ages were dark and long. The age before was greater in its pagan glory, the age since is greater in its Christian glory; and you can easily understand, I think, that the Middle Ages, the one thousand years b. c., was just the sorrowful battle time in the world between Pagan truth and Christian truth, between man-made truth and God's truth.

You know when a little Christian truth comes into your own young hearts it generally is born of a little battle you have had with a falsehood or with a bit of selfishness. So it is with the history of Christian truth everywhere, in all places and at all times.

We people are living now in the New Time already four hundred years old, and we must be as true to our Time as others have been to theirs. We need not make any more mistakes, we can see and read and write and ride, and can do everything in the world we wish to do, just so it is not wrong.

So let the new Colombo boy and girl dare to dream and do as truly as Columbus did. Light is fully come. Room is fully come. Learning and goodness are still coming. Let us all discover all we can, for the light that now is, is neither dark nor pagan.

V.

Colombo went to live in Portugal, probably, just as young men and young women nowadays come to live in cities. Whether it is best and wisest to do so or not, each young or old person must decide for himself. No preaching on the subject will enlighten any one in particular. We only know it was like Colombo carefully to find out for himself, what was best, and he went in 1470, and found Portugal to be the center of life in culture and enterprise. The wise Prince Henry had lived twenty years before, and his great attention to navigation had made it the leading nation in this.

Colombo seemed to bid farewell to his beloved Genoa, as she faded in her glory on the waters, and to take up his home with the new life which belonged to Portugal, as she spread her sails out in new discoveries. No other nation was doing anything like it.

Perhaps Colombo's brother Bartholomew was already at Lisbon when he came there, and was engaged in the business of making maps and selling books; at least this is what Colombo did, when he came, whether he was in partnership with his brother or not. He made enough money in this book business to live, and to send something to his father, for he never forgot his father; but he probably read more of his books than he sold.

Books were then, of course, great wonders. They were yet a very expensive luxury, and only the dukes and dignitaries could afford to buy them. Colombo, however, seems to have managed to have them to read by going into the business himself.

Colombo probably did not have an extended business in this line, for he failed to become very rich; he seemed to gravitate to his old life of navigation. He also fell in love with an old navigator's daughter, or rather, she

He Falls in Love.

fell first in love with him. As soon as Colombo was a citizen of Lisbon he was an attendant at church. This devoted and upright and handsome young Italian with his face set toward true things in a strange country, was very likely to attract the attention of some true young lady, and so he did. She was an inmate of the convent, and "sought him with such expressions of affection that he easily yielded to her charms," and they were married.

The young man probably had other plans and heard other voices than the voice of love, in his wide outlook upon his manhood, with all its grand possibilities in that time and place, but he rightfully yielded to a true love, and it blessed him.

One thing we know, it blessed him by bringing to him more books and plans on navigation. Her father or grandfather (history is all mixed up about which he was) had been a great Portuguese navigator, Perestrello by name. Her name was Phelipa Moniz Perestrello, with a Dona before it, which meant that she was a young lady of rank. Don and Dona were titles that stood for much in Spain and Portugal.

Columbo seems to have always had a way of interesting people of rank. Though he was himself born with no rank but that of a fine physique and a noble spirit, he always ranked rightly with the noble of blood. He naturally belonged to the people of refinement and power.

This young pair, when married, went with her mother—her father was dead—to live away out in the ocean on an island called Porto Santo. I told you to remember this island, and I hope you have, for it was the romantic home of this charming couple.

There they lived, for it was where the bride owned some property, and there Colombo studied Perestrello's maps and plans, and charts (for he was still going to school). He was where he could hear and see the latest things going on in Portuguese discoveries, which were at this time most active. The beating and the roar of the mighty Ocean Sea about his very home in the night and in the day, must have filled him with its majesty, and no doubt he grew more and more to feel at home with it. A little boy was born there. His name was Diego,— Don Diego he is called in after history.

Baby Diego.

Those were peaceful days for Colombo. He had enough to live on without much concern. He studied and talked and loved his little family (for he was always passionately fond of all his family connections), while coming to a solid conclusion that the mystery of darkness could and must be solved.

About this time, Colombo heard of a man by the name of Toscanelli, a man then about seventy-seven years old, who lived at Florence,

Italy. In fact a great many people had heard of him, for he had long before made himself famous, in that slow-going day, by writing a little book on what he believed the world was like. He thought there was a way to that wonderful India in the East, not by going east over dreadful mountains and long distances, but by going west around the world, on water, and coming to the East. There lay the water toward the west, why not try it? This was very startling, for Toscanelli was a great scholar. He had really written a letter to King Alphonzo, King of Portugal, once upon a time, giving his views definitely, and had also sent him a map of what he believed the West was like. The Portuguese were for years greatly excited about it, but the excitement did n't come to anything after all, because nobody wanted to try it.

Dr. Paul Toscanelli.

Colombo, however, heard about that Toscanelli, and since, as I said before, Colombo seemed to belong to scholars and to what they knew, he dared to write to the great old Doctor. He had a fine handwriting always (the lack of which has spoiled many a young man's good start in the world), and he could write a most interesting letter. He wrote, asking Toscanelli for a copy of the letter he had heard of, and also for the map which he had once sent to the king. It was asking a good deal, it seems to me, but the Doctor granted his request and sent them both to him, giving his exact calculations. This was a great compliment to our sincere and energetic Colombo, for he was only a plain young man, as yet, thinking in the same great lines. It was all a most important success for him. This same map went with him through all his further difficulties and successes, until he actually touched our shores ten or fifteen years afterward. Uunfortunately, however, it was lost after that.

This map, when Colombo first received it,

must have stirred his blood, for it taught exactly what he thought, except that he believed the ocean was narrower than Toscanelli planned. It calculated that the earth (if round) must be about eighteen thousand miles in circumference. You know now it is twenty-five thousand miles. How would you like to sail out on such a mistake as that? But this map suited Colombo the best of anything he had ever seen. He thought eighteen thousand miles to be the circumference, yet he believed the continent—nobody supposed for a minute there were two continents—took up more space than Toscanelli thought it did. He believed there was less ocean. Toscanelli said the land occupied about two-thirds of the circumference. Here is an example in fractions:— two-thirds of eighteen thousand miles = twelve thousand miles. He thought that must be the size of the land on the earth, which, you see, left six thousand miles of water.

Colombo thought the unknown waters were not so wide and that the land was much wider, and this was the best geography the world had, until Columbus solved the mystery. No wonder it helped to break up those awful Dark Ages.

There were other great men and things helping him on, you know. About this time, Colombo had some corre-
Leonardo Da Vinci. spondence with the great genius, Leonardo Da Vinci, who was interested in more different things than almost any other person who ever lived. From being the inventor of the wheelbarrow to painting some of the greatest pictures in the world, his mind was one which allowed nothing to escape him.

So, in great art galleries, when you see pictures by Da Vinci, just remember that he had a good word to put into Colombo's head about that western way to the East.

The astrolabe was an instrument with which men measured the height of the sun from the horizon, at this time, and it, as well as the compass, enabled men to cut loose and sail out of sight of land.

The years were going by with Colombo, and these facts tempted him more and more to try the deep—while very few others thought anything about it.

He sailed often on the Guinea coast. Perhaps he made the trip to Iceland at this time.

He was a gray-haired man when but thirty years old. It is said "his whole countenance had an air of authority." He must have had a most striking appearance, for he had large blue eyes, was very erect and tall; and to have an air of authority along with gray hairs, and all that with a disposition "engaging and affable," and to be simple in diet and dress—this makes a combination most rare.

Appearance of Columbo.

It is not surprising, however, that we have no portrait of Columbus—only as some one has imagined him to appear—for the world was only then beginning to paint portraits. Of course only great people had them, and painters never thought of Colombo being great.

Remember, also, that not until 1839 were pictures "taken" by any process except by painting. Now we have them for a few dollars a dozen.

Colombo was simple in dress, when gorgeousness was the fashion; not self-indulgent in eating or drinking, when that has always been the fashion—these things mark him a hero, in the beginning; though his poverty, like many another person's, may have greatly aided his heroism.

Our Colombo gradually rose in life, in spite of all his difficulties — perhaps it would be better to say he rose by them, for if a character is great enough to "stand the strain of life" at all, God generally makes more character by more strain, until He has one to be depended upon. Boys know how this is when they want to make more muscle. It is by exercise. This character that was being formed at Portugal in those years of strain and trial, through much exercise of discouragement and encouragement, rising and falling, was the very character God could depend upon when it came to the test in after years.

His maps did n't pay very well but he somehow could approach kings, and write to great painters and great doctors and have great schemes. He had risen, at last, to where he succeeded in having his plan carefully laid before King John of Portugal.

This most cultivated and learned nation in navigation, this center of much new learning, where Colombo had struggled to live for twelve or fifteen years, now faced its chance for life, but how little it dreamed it had anything to learn from this self-taught Genoese! We do not know many particulars about

King John of Portugal.

it all, only that King John did give enough attention to it once upon a time, to appoint a lot of men to look into the matter and decide. Colombo was asked to loan them his charts and plans so that the Council might better understand exactly what his scheme was, and before he received them again they had secretly sent a caravel out into the deep to see how this very visionary notion might work.

They found out nothing, of course, because Colombo himself was not along, and the very wise (?) Council reported Colombo's plans a great failure. Now just think! They had as much, and a great deal more, than Colombo, to go by. They had Toscanelli's ideas. They had done a great deal of discovering before. They had vessels and money and men and experience, but all that did not make a character strong enough to "get there." No, they reported it all a failure— and were not ashamed of doing so.

But Colombo, instead of feeling mortified and discouraged, and giving up his scheme, though he was in debt and alone, seemed to be only more determined. He was now sure he knew more about it than they all, and the next we hear of him he has quietly left Lisbon.

Colombo Leaves Portugal.

Whether he leaves because they make such sport of him or whether it is because he is much in debt and has to leave, we do not know. We can only learn that he went without people knowing where or when. But there is' one sure thing, the next King of Portugal very politely asked him, in after years, to come back again, and said that everything should be made right, and that they might give him what he wanted. But it was too late then.

Colombo took his little boy (and he must have packed up the map, too) and went away. The loving young wife, with whom he had shared a home so happily, had probably died.

It must have been a sad breaking up of his fond dreams of what the Portuguese were, and of what they could do. They were making such great discoveries down the African coast and everywhere close to shore—and were the only nation doing such things—and if Colombo had been made of weaker stuff, his heart would have broken, and he would have died (for he could n't give it up) and that would have been all.

Then my story would have ended here. Instead of that, just think what he did! He was so sure of his great thought, that he only felt sorry and angry with Portugal because she was to be left out of this great plan. He slipped off alone.

How little it appeared to be that way! How it took a great soul to know it! So it is now and always has been. Only the great of faith have eyes to see things as they really are. The rest of the world follow some leader in a round ring, like little children at a game of some sort, while those who know something can be done, and must be done, *just go and do it.*

These are the noble of God's world, who reach so far into the unknown that they have no other hand to lead them but God's hand. God made it all and knows it all, and it will not do to ask men much about it, sometimes.

So Columbus felt that Portugal was left forlorn and alone, and so she was, when he left her himself; but he took with him all that Portugal could give him, and that which Portugal knew about discovery, and his maps and his little boy.

VI.

After Portugal was left by Columbus, what did he do? He never gave up, but only wondered what other nation under the sun would undertake the great business that he knew must be done.

No other nation knew as much about discovery as did Portugal, so it was with him a most solemn question as to what next he should do and where next he should go. This is probably the time when he sent his brother Bartholomew to England to offer his project to Henry VII.

We know his brother went to England at some time on this errand, and stayed so long — earning his living, no doubt, while trying to interest somebody—that when he returned, Columbus had already gone for the second time under Spain. There were no newspapers

England's Chance.

in those days, to tell all the news, so it must have been a great surprise to him to find Columbus gone, for it is said he had with him a favorable proposition from King Henry VII. of England.

Perhaps Columbus went to his own city of Genoa at this time, to ask the Genoese to undertake it, but all is uncertainty as to exactly when Columbus gave England and Genoa the grand opportunity to carry out his plan.

He thought of France, no doubt, at this time, for France was a strong power, now under Louis XI., and had Genoa by the neck, but France was not the nation to undertake a thing like this for she had done nothing in the way of discovery.

In those days of little acquaintance between nations, and when news and gossip traveled slowly, Columbus probably knew little about the real disposition of any country until he had lived in it. He was utterly alone. He was "a man without a country," that is, he was really not at home in any of them. He was, indeed, the first American, for he was related to all countries. He was an Italian, that is, a Genoese, and Genoa had come to be quite French; he had adopted Portugal as his home, and he was thus a part of those three countries. It yet remains for me to tell you of how he became related to Spain, and finally to America.

When he became a Spaniard in order to gain great Spain, how little she realized that she gained more than he did.

Nothing is known of his wanderings, at first, but it is found that he came into Spain and laid all his plans before two large-hearted, wealthy Spanish noblemen, who, in some way, entertained him as their guest for two years. They were the Duke of Medina Sidonia, and the Duke of Medina Celi.

They lived down on the southern coast of Spain, directly south of Portugal, facing the great ocean. They were immensely wealthy, and they must have been much pleased with the princely Columbus, though all he had was a princely plan and a little boy. They, at least, treated him royally, and finally at the end of two years, gave him a letter of introduction to their Queen—Isabella, the Queen of Spain. This is how Columbus first came to know this important person.

The Dukes of Sidonia and Celi.

These noblemen thought very seriously about undertaking the voyage for themselves, as they were well able, but they finally concluded it was a matter of too great importance, and that it should be done by a nation instead of by private persons, for Columbus had them well under the influence of his enthusiasm, you see. They wrote to the Queen that they, themselves, had thought of fitting Columbus out for his voyage, but that in case of important discoveries, only some monarch would be able to command the countries found. Yet they wished to keep an interest in the business and have some of the good of it.

All this introduction to the Queen and King of Spain was pushed right along after the dukes gave up carrying out the plan themselves. Columbus had made up his mind to go to France, but the dukes could not let this opportunity to do something great in discovery pass from their own country; they must have written a very interesting letter to the Queen about Columbus, in order to have it interest her so much as it did, and at a time when she must have been one of the most occupied persons in the world.

She was a young mother of young children, and had much to take up her mind in managing her wily husband—whom she always loved and served in the highest sense. She was also so absorbed in managing her realm in the fear of God, that she sometimes had to lead armies herself. How could she stop to become acquainted with a wandering stranger, with a most strange scheme? But she did, and requested that he be presented to her. It was a most unfortunately busy time, however.

Before we go any farther we must know something about Isabella and Ferdinand, and about Spain—for you will see plenty of Spanish relations at our great World's Fair party.

Isabella.

Isabella, next to Columbus himself, is the most important relative we have.

Isabella and Ferdinand were at Cordova when Columbus first came to them. Look at the map and see what journey he and his little boy took, bearing the important letter of introduction. (Some writers say Columbus was first introduced to the King and Queen of Spain by Perez, the Prior of the Convent of La Rabida, but this is a mistake. This interesting introduction through Perez came later.)

When Columbus first saw Queen Isabella, she was about thirty-four years of age. She was a very beautiful woman, and a very Queen, indeed.

She was a descendant of John of Gaunt, through both her parents, and was a woman of very strong character. This showed itself to be true when she was but a young girl, thirteen years old. Her father, King John II., of Castile, had died when she was three years old, leaving his crown to Henry, his son, who was only a half-brother to Isabella, and who was old enough to have daughters of his own. Then there was another brother, so there was little chance that she would ever be Queen, yet her hand was sought in marriage, when she was but eleven years old, for Ferdinand, Prince of Aragon, whom she did finally marry, after many difficulties, at eighteen years of age. Instead of becoming betrothed to Ferdinand at eleven years of age, she was betrothed to his brother Carlos, who was forty years old. Fortunately, he died, and then in a year she was betrothed to another man; but the young miss refused to be bestowed in this manner, upon any one, without consulting "the nobles of the realm." Many things stirred the people against the king, her half-brother, who was not a good man, and they raised an army to have his brother made king, instead. So Henry then thought he could straighten out matters by having Isabella marry a horrible old man by the name of Don Pedro Girou. Isabella was very miserable about this, but the betrothal was made. She said she would not marry him, but that she should plunge a dagger into his heart if she was forced to do so. (She was now but fifteen years old, and had been betrothed three times to men whom she hated.) But in spite of her threat, Grand Master Don Pedro was on his way to be married to her when he suddenly died. Is it not rather remarkable how this lovely, brave young woman was thus saved to become the wife of the man she so loved always!

After this last man died, the king's brother died, the one whom the people were striving to have take the crown from Henry. So they now offered to fight to have young Isabella, the half-sister, made Queen.

She said, "No, she would not be Queen of Castile until it was her right and duty to be Queen," but she and the people forced old Henry to sign an agreement that she should be heir to the crown instead of his own children (who really were not heirs), and also an agreement that she should have the right to choose her own husband.

So she finally lived in peace, and at eighteen, she chose young Ferdinand of Aragon to be her husband, but they had an exciting time getting married in secret, for old Henry, who paid no attention to his agreement, had an army trying to prevent the wedding. He failed, and died soon after. Then Isabella was really Queen of Castile and Leon. Ferdinand agreed, when he married her, that she should retain all her sovereignty. This was a most important matter, later, when Isabella became interested in our Columbus.

Queen at Last.

Isabella was a devout Christian, and had a most loving and tender heart; all her bitter, unnatural duties finally broke her heart, for she died when only fifty-three years old, having lived and loved through great wars and family anxieties. But she was always cheerful and lovely in character and in person. She is described as being very beautiful in form and face; of medium height, with fair complexion; her hair of a bright chestnut color, inclining to red, and mild blue eyes beaming with intelligence and sensibility. She was exceedingly beautiful—" The handsomest lady," says one of her household, " whom I ever beheld, and the most gracious in manners."

"She was dignified and modest, even to a degree of reserve. She early imbibed a relish for letters, in which she was superior to Ferdinand." At the same time we read of her playfulness, and joy in recreation with her family as they grew into young manhood and womanhood, which sometimes quite troubled the very pious advisers that she had. Her influence as a Queen and a mother has been felt in the whole world, perhaps as no other one woman's ever has been. Queen Elizabeth was great as a Queen, but not as a woman; she, also, had very much to do with settling this New World, and is one of our relatives, but Isabella was not only Queen, but the mother of beautiful Queens; one of them was the good Queen Catherine of England. She had five children; the two eldest, Isabella and Juan, the most promising and gifted of the family, died as they reached mature life, instead of living to carry out the greatness of Spain, which Ferdinand and Isabella had so wisely begun.

I have introduced you to Isabella and Ferdinand, so now an introduction to Spain comes next.

What Made Spain.

Castile and Leon were married to Aragon, you see, when Isabella married Ferdinand. This young King and Queen were very active and soon added more provinces to their kingdom. That is what made Spain.

They felt their great mission in the world was to use their combined power to convert the world to the church, at least, to convert all in their own domain. The church, to them, was the power of God in the world. If this was true, then it was supposed to be their duty either to convert everybody or to drive them out of the country, for

God was the ruler, and all must obey Him. So they carried on those terrible "pious wars" against the Moors and against the Jews, and dealt most severely with all who doubted the church.

It was a most sickening piece of business, and one which finally, it seems to me, broke Isabella's heart.

The Inquisition was revived during their reign, and hundreds of thousands were tortured to death for not believing in the church. It was all because the world had not yet learned that God was Love. It was supposed that God only ruled by power and blood, and they had not yet learned the rule of love. We must not judge too harshly, for we do not yet know much about love, ourselves.

Spain was coming to her greatest glory, and was ending her wars triumphantly, about the time she came to know our Columbus. Isabella and Ferdinand had been married about twenty years, and they had encouraged art and literature, and reformed laws and had governed their united realm with wonderful wisdom and power. Spain was the greatest nation of Europe at this time. She was not so cultivated as Portugal, nor so advanced in discovery and in learning, but she was greatest in size, and in power to conquer the world. And now, just as the fiercest wars were going on with the Moors, when Isabella herself had sometimes to wear a soldier's suit and command armies, while King Ferdinand was in command somewhere else; and just as they were beginning to believe they would finally conquer, and when the court, with all its splendid array, was sort of camping around through the domain of Spain, there came a poor man with a letter of introduction from somebody, about a plan of his which Portugal had tried and believed worth nothing.

Spain in Her Glory.

"What!" said everybody, "does that fellow suppose this whole grand time of triumphs, marchings and music, is all going to stop, so he may have a chance to make himself glorious? No, indeed!"

Yes, it was a most sad time for a man like Columbus to put in an appearance with anything on hand but to help fight the Moors. The Moors, the Moors must go! The religion of Christ must triumph! That was the business of the world just then.

And Columbus himself was such a loyal son of the church that he did not doubt that was true. He loved the church and wanted to see the church conquer. He asked no questions about theology but took theology as he found it. He felt the church to be the all-glorious and beautiful hope of God in the world. He believed in obeying God, if it took his life, and he was ready to lay down his life for the truth as he understood it.

Columbus and the Church.

Sometime, during his six years' waiting upon the court of Spain, Columbus seems to have found a new wife. Her name was Beatriz Enriquez. She was young and very beautiful and of a noble family. Her brothers were always good friends to Columbus, and finally went on the great voyage.

Beatriz Enriquez.

Another little boy was born; his name was Fernando, and he was a dear son along with Diego. He it was who grew up to be a very scholarly man and wrote his father's history.

Columbus, while waiting for Isabella and Ferdinand to make up their minds as to what they should do for him, joined the army and helped to fight the Moors. He heard how they held that wonderful holy city of Jerusalem, the very place where Christ was crucified, and he heard how Queen Isabella had embroidered a most beautiful veil with her own hands, to be sent to the holy place as soon as it was taken from the Moors, and all these things made him more and more sure that some day, God would have control of this whole world. It would seem that just such a King and Queen ought to rule this world for God.

While waiting and hoping that Isabella and Ferdinand would come to help him get hold of the whole New World for God, he would sometimes become dreadfully discouraged, but they still put him off, saying they would try to hear all about his plan some other time.

Once they said, "Yes, we will have this thing seen to," and one winter up at Salamanca, where there were a great University and a great many learned and wise men, and where the Queen was spending the winter, they concluded they would give this Columbus a chance to tell his story, and would have a

Council of Salamanca.

Council called to examine him and really settle this matter.

But Talavera was confessor to the Queen, and he had his mind made up that it was foolish for the Queen to be so interested in a crazy man, a man who was about fifty years old, and who had so far failed in life; and as she was so very conscientious and careful always to obey her God through her confessor, it is a great wonder indeed that she had such strong, natural, womanly sense as to think anything at all about Columbus.

But Talavera got up the Council of Salamanca, and, of course, he called a Council that suited himself, and for several years it would not say yes or no. There happened to be one or two men in it, however, who held on to the hope that the world might be round, and that Columbus might be right; yet, at last, it gave the decision that the whole scheme was "vain, impracticable, and resting on grounds too weak to merit the support of the government."

This sounds very grand and dignified. Poor Queen Isabella and Columbus; they must have wondered if it could be possible that they were only dreamers and schemers, and that 'the great Council was all-wise!

How sad to be so mistaken! How sorry the Queen must have been for the noble and handsome hero, whom she felt in her heart was wiser than all the confessors and wise men.

Two men of the Council supported the scheme—Cardinal Mendoza, and the Archbishop of Seville. They were both important men. They managed to have the King and Queen answer Columbus that, "although they were too much occupied at present to embark in his undertaking, yet at the conclusion of the war, they would find both time and inclination to treat with him."

This is carefully said. They do not say

they'll find time and inclination to undertake for him, but time and inclination to "treat with him."

So, after six years' waiting, fighting, and living, sometimes upon the Queen's money, and sometimes without any money, Columbus concludes if this is all he has gained, he will leave Spain, just as he left Portugal, and find out again, "what next."

VII.

How bitterly the discussions all came up again, about the world being round, for these Churchmen attacked Colon (let us call our hero Colon for a little while, for this was his name in Spanish) on Scriptural ground. To say the world was round, was to say the Bible was not true. The Bible said a great deal about the four corners of the earth, and about the sea being spread out as molten glass, etc., etc.; how could the sea be flat and yet round?

None of these things puzzled Colon. His scientific turn of mind did not see things as they appeared. In his inherent greatness he could see farther than they in their learned greatness. He could feel man's smallness and God's greatness, and that God might have made a ball so big that when he put little man on it there was no up nor down to it, if only man and beast, and water, and everything else stayed on it; that was all the "down" there was to anything connected with the great round earth. So he was not worried about anything of that kind, or about the Bible either. He was only troubled about unlearning some of their learning.

Colon left the court folks and started for France at last, in good earnest. He and his son Diego next appeared at **The Convent of La Rabida and Juan Perez.** the gate of a convent, which received its name from some miraculous claim in its very early day, of having cured the dreadful disease of hydrophobia. Our Lady of the Madness was its patron saint.

It has been a most puzzling matter as to when this visit to the convent was made.

We have adopted the theory of the later writers — who must all necessarily go to

Navarrete, and to the testimony of Fernandez in the famous lawsuit,—that this is the first visit which Columbus made to the convent, with a "little boy," and "in distress." From all that can be gathered, it is thought that this "little boy" was about twelve years old.

It was situated in a lovely spot, and here was where Juan Perez had retired from this same court, disgusted, or at least, tired of court life.

He had been confessor to the Queen, and yet without airs or self-glory about that, he lived here so plainly and simply that he had plenty of time and heart to hear all that this stranger with the "little boy" had to tell him about his mission in the world.

How sweetly God plans things sometimes! This ex-confessor to the Queen had much less to do with the powers at the court at present, than the confessor Talavera, and he had learned to live without any of its dazzling glory, a true, simple life where he could do most good; yet how sweet and just like true things, that seem to happen sometimes, for him, instead of Talavera, really to be the one who, at last, should win the Queen to her decision.

It was this way. Colon was hungry, and poor, and alone, indeed. His little boy must have something to eat, and Colon knew about the hospitality of the convents, which were situated here and there in the country, so he went to La Rabida and asked for bread and water.

Juan Perez saw that he was entertaining a man of great genius. In a little while he was all awake to what **Garcia Fernandez.** seemed to him to be a very important matter. He soon found a learned young man who helped to talk over this wonderful scheme with Columbus. This young man's name was Garcia Fernandez—he was the village doctor. The village was only down the hill from the convent and no doubt these three had a grand and exciting visit together, very soon.

At last—at last, Colon had found some one who would listen to him without thinking he was crazy. This Convent dedicated to Our Lady of the Madness seems to have been the only spot on earth where this man, accused of madness, had a chance to lay his head.

Real friendliness at last grasped Columbus by the hand and opened its heart to do anything in the world that could be done.

They talked and planned and figured up all the knowledge they could get together, as fast as possible, for Colon, who was now fifty-seven years old, was so determined to go to France that no time was to be lost.

Between them they commanded a great deal of learning, for it was the kind that was real, and the kind that could thrive away off there in the country by the Sea, by itself; it was not that sort which paraded itself on nothing, in great councils and before great folks. Garcia Fernandez and Juan Perez had plenty of books and knew them. They were men who looked out of their own eyes straight into that sincere man's eyes who had dreamed his dream so long, and had also seen through his own eyes all his life; so they three, together, saw something mighty.

Now there were two other wonderful pairs of seeing eyes in the world, about this same time, who felt just what these men thought. These were Isabella's and those of her best friend, the Marchioness Moya.

Perez knew them well, not as court ladies, but as women. He had known the Queen most intimately, and he knew he commanded her highest respect, and that anything he might chance to choose, she would, in her wisdom, believe was the best choice. So what do you think! Juan Perez borrowed a mule of a man by the name of Juan Rodesquez, and started at midnight to go two hundred miles to see the Queen, expecting to change her mind, after all that had been done.

The Midnight Ride.

This is the kind of desperate earnestness that moves something when it starts out to do it. Here was a plain man, superior of a country convent, hoping to do that which some of the greatest people in the realm had failed to do, and that was to win the court to favor this project.

He started at midnight so as not to arouse the suspicions of this little gossipy town of Palos, and because he was in the greatest haste.

Colon waited at the convent, wondering, indeed, what next, and he must have actually rested as he had not before in years. In due time the prior came back with word from the Queen that she must again see him, and he brought with him over two hundred dollars for Colon to buy for himself a court suit. He brought also a mule to be his very own. Mules, in those days, were fine things to have, and not everybody owned one to ride. They were worth from three hundred to four hundred dollars. Colon then took the new suit of fine clothes and got astride his own mule and started to see the beautiful Queen once again.

Another Mule Ride.

These three men had made up their minds as to about what the terms should be. Colon was to ask for three vessels, and for men, and for one-eighth of the profits, and that he should be Admiral of the little fleet and should be appointed Governor of the lands he should discover, the title to come down to his heirs after him.

These terms depended entirely upon his success, except the start. The starting out was surely a small expense, only three little boats and the men and the necessary provisions!

But it is very surprising that the wiseheads, Ferdinand especially, thought *if* Columbus discovered something, there was going to be "too much in it" for himself. Queen Isabella pleaded that it was all fair. The Marchioness, her best friend, also pleaded for Colon. But no! another Council was called, and other wise heads said the plan might be good enough, but Colon asked for too much glory and profit.

It is very strange that even men of to-day can draw conclusions as foolish as those men did, after it has been proven that Colon did not ask too much. One writer says, "His arrogant spirit led him to magnify his own importance before he had proved it. He failed in modesty," etc., while the truth is, he showed a mighty wisdom in not going about

Envy and Bitterness.

the thing half-hearted. What would have been the outcome, if, with a weak "modesty," he had asked for half enough?

But the authorities said it was too much, so Colon acceded somewhat, and offered to bear one-eighth the expense.

No, that would n't do. So Colon simply left again. He mounted his gift of a mule and I suppose he thanked his stars that Isabella was his friend, at least; but he had gone only two miles when a man came after him, post haste, and said, "Come back. The Queen herself will furnish everything asked for."

The Queen Will Do It.

The story used to be that she offered her jewels, but it seems that is not quite true; but it is true that she said she would, on her own responsibility, give Columbus all the support he asked for, and that she, as Queen of Castile, would supply him the means. This relieved Ferdinand from responsibility, though the money was at first borrowed from his treasury and he and she together signed the great and important papers that at last gave to Columbus his wish—the chance to sail out on the Sea of Darkness.

Now was the time for his heart to fail if there was any fail in him, for now it must be proven that he was right. He had offered all that a man could offer and that was his life. Now he was actually to give it.

The very important paper making this "pauper pilot" an Admiral of the Ocean Sea, and giving him authority to govern whatever he should discover was signed, *"This seventeenth day of April, in the year of the Birth of our Saviour Jesus Christ, one thousand four hundred and ninety-two, in this city of Santa Fè, in the Plain of Grenada."*

The whole paper is not very long, but it is very formal and has many big words in it, so I will not trouble you to read it now.

The most curious part of all, though, was

the letter written by Ferdinand and Isabella to the great Kubla Khan and to Prestor John, for "*Christopher Columbus, who will tell them that they are in good health and perfect prosperity,*" to take with him when he should find himself in their great kingdoms. This letter was written April 30, only thirteen days after the great document was signed.

How little any of them thought that that poor letter was going to be dragged up and down and around the wilds of our New Continent while men were hunting for the Khan and his mountains of pearls, and cities where parties were given to ten thousand people at one time, everybody dressed in cloth of gold! No, that letter never reached Kubla Kahn, it only reached our wild Indians.

Now Colon started immediately with his letters in his pockets for the homelike convent, and how like a man of to-day he

was in that sleepy Spanish world. He
expected to be off in *ten days!* Was not
Colon a real American for "hust-
A Real American. ling," when he had a chance to
"hustle," and yet was he not
magnificently patient when he must be
patient? How long he had waited, and
now what haste!

The King and Queen had a claim on two
vessels which belonged to the Port of Palos,
so they gave Colon an order to take those
two vessels and their crews, and to find
also another one for his voyage. Orders
were sent to the Mayor of Palos to collect
men and provisions and arms and all that
was necessary for the voyage, and a morning was appointed when this Mayor was—
to have the orders published in the morning
papers? No, to read them to the towns-
people in St. George's Church. And O!
into what an excitement the poor little
town was thrown! It was dreadful news.

Everybody was so astonished to think this stranger that had been around of late had gotten them all into such great difficulty. Nobody would go. The order from the court then said that they must go—that prisoners could be pardoned of their crimes if they would go, yet there were not enough.

Yes, it was a sad day for Palos, and the business of getting off was so dreadful that it seemed almost an impossibility. The month of May passed away and Colon was uneasy and in haste and hard at work. June came and was almost gone when a man arrived with word direct from the court that if it was necessary, the military forces would see that Colon had his men; that is, there would be war, if necessary, to make somebody go.

A Sad Day for Palos.

This frightened the people still more, and it began to be a very serious matter. The good Perez finally succeeded in interesting in the scheme, two men, brothers, who were quite willing to enter into it if there was really anything to be gained; but they, like every one, supposed it was only a crazy dream. But when Colon gave them all his thoughts in the matter, and told them of all that he expected to gain for Spain and for everybody who would enter into the undertaking, they became quite willing to go. Their names were Martin Alonzo Pinzon and Yanez Pinzon. They agreed to go, to manage the two small boats, the "Nina" and the "Pinta," which were there in port. They were the leading men of the community and it was quite a victory when they really decided to join Colon.

The Pinzons.

After many difficulties, another vessel was found, which was larger and had a deck. This was the "Santa Maria," and Columbus was very busy getting these boats into a very safe condition, and July was gone and

August had come, before all was ready, the morning of the third of August. It was Friday and there was no sleep in all that town the night before. The men who were ready to go numbered one hundred and twenty. Ninety were rough men. The others were priests, a secretary, and an attorney, some physicians, captains and pilots.

Colon was in command of the "Santa Maria." The Pinzons commanded the other two vessels. All were at St. George's Church to have their sins absolved and to be ready to sail long before day. It was more like one grand funeral of the whole town than anything else. There had been many vessels sail from this shady little port before, but nothing like this had ever started out.

This sad, glad, wonderful new thought, at last sailed out of the harbor and turned west for the great Gibraltar and for the Ocean Sea by the time the sun was up, and the little town settled down, as best it could, to wonder about all the strange things that were going on in the world.

The good Queen Isabella took young Diego into her own family, to be a page to her young son, Prince Juan.

VIII.

We will begin this voyage with Columbus' own words, for they are the introduction to his journal which he kept while he made the path through the strange Ocean Sea of Darkness.

It is easy to note from them that his first, supreme motive, at that time, was to take Christianity to a perishing world. He had seen Christianity conquer the Moors and Jews in Spain; that is, he had seen what the world then thought was Christian conquest. Mohammedanism falling before Christianity as it did in 1492 before Columbus' very eyes, made him feel very sure that Christ was about to conquer the world in this way. We have learned better, but we must humbly remember how we have learned it through others.

Columbus had read in Marco Polo how the Kubla Khan desired to learn of Christianity; for if he read the book at all, and we know he did, he must have read the request (from the Khan) that the Pope " would send a hundred men of learning, thoroughly acquainted with the principles of the Christian religion, as well as with the seven arts, and qualified to prove to the learned of his dominions, by just and fair argument, that the faith professed by Christians is superior to, and founded upon more evident truth than any other; that the gods of the Tartars and the idols worshiped in their houses were only evil spirits." He also wanted brought to him some of the " holy oil from the lamp which is kept burning over the sepulchre of our Lord Jesus Christ." No doubt Columbus wished he could take some of this with him.

Columbus himself seems to have informed the King and Queen of this desire of the Khan and his successors, as you will see. His story begins, "In the name of Jesus Christ." This sentence is remarkably simple when compared with other documents of the day. Jesus Christ and all his attributes, God and all his power, were dragged out in words and words at the beginning of every important writing. In fact, it was thought very impolite to mention any name that was at all revered, without also mentioning the reverence in which it was held.

Columbus goes on,—"Most High, most Christian, most excellent and most mighty Princes, King and Queen of Spain and of the islands of the sea, our lord and our sovereign, this present year, 1492, after Your Highness had put an end to the war against the Moors, who were reigning in Europe, and had terminated the great war in the city of Granada, where this present year, the second day of the month of January, I saw floating the royal banners of your Highness on the towers of the Alhambra, the fortress of the said city, and where I saw the Moorish King come to the gates of the city and kiss the royal hands of your Highness and of my lord, the Prince! Then in this present month and according to the information which I had given to your Highness of the lands of India, and of a Prince called Grand Khan, which means, in our common language, King of Kings, and that several times he and his predecessors had sent to Rome to demand Doctors in our Holy Faith to teach him; as the Holy Father had never provided any, and as so many people were being lost in their idolatrous sects of perdition, your Highnesses thought, in your position as Christian Catholics and as amiable princes and propagators of the holy Christian Faith and as enemies of the sects of Mohammedanism and of all idolatries and heresies, of sending me, Christopher Columbus, to the said Countries of India to see the said princes and the peoples and the countries and their dispositions and the state of everything, and the manner in which one could best set about their conversion to holy faith. You commanded me not to go to the Orient by land, as was the custom to do, but, on the contrary, to take the western route by which we have no positive knowledge of any one ever having passed. Consequently, after having chased all the Jews from your kingdoms and domains, your Highness commanded me, in this same month of January, to set out with a fleet sufficiently large, for the said countries of India. And on that occasion you granted me great favors and ennobled me, inasmuch that henceforth I was called Don, and was Grand Admiral of the Ocean Sea, and Viceroy and perpetual Governor of all the islands and mainlands of which I should make the discovery and conquest, and by which, in consequence, the discovery and conquest may be made [See the man's faith!] in the Ocean Sea, and you decreed that my oldest son should succeed me and that it should be thus from generation to generation forever and forever. I started from the city of Granada, Saturday, the 12th of the month of May, of this same year, 1492. I came to the city of Palos, a seaport where I fitted up three vessels very convenient for such an undertaking, and I left the harbor very well provided with a great many provisions and seamen. Friday, the 3d day of August of said year, and half an hour before sunrise, I followed the route of the Canary Islands, which belong to your Highness and which are situated in said Ocean Sea, to take from there my route and to sail until I should arrive at the Indies, so as to acquit myself of the embassy of your Highness to these princes and thus to execute what you thus commanded me to do. I intend, also, on this account, to record very punctually and to relate day by day all that I may do and see and all that happen to me, as will be seen farther on. Moreover, Mighty Prince and Princess, purposing to write each night that which shall have happened in the day and each day the navigation of the night, I intend, besides, to make a new marine map, on which I shall indicate the situation of all the sea and of all the lands of the Ocean Sea in their proper position, and the direction in which the wind comes to them, and to compose a book in which I shall represent in painting the latitude from the equinoctial line, and the longitude from the west line. It is very especially important that I forget sleep and that I study with perseverance my navigation, to fulfill all the obligations that are imposed on me, which will be a great labor."

These are what I call most majestic words. Columbus has been represented as here saying he should not sleep until he had found land, which you can see would be only foolish talk. He did not say that, for the above translation has been carefully made from Las Casas, who has preserved it for us in Columbus' own words. It is just as he wrote it, and is the whole of what he wrote as an introduction to his journal. He then begins again by saying,—" I started Friday, August 3d, from the shoals of the Saltes and we made before sunset sixty miles, then we went single file towards the southwest."

Sad, sweet picture this is, of the little fleet, as night came on, heading single file for the great unknown, loaded with such great responsibilities. Many of its men never saw Spain again.

This first voyage across the Atlantic was made in three small vessels no larger than the yachts which now go from one point to another along the coast; rarely do they venture across the ocean in these days. However, Columbus did wisely, it is said, in choosing small vessels. They were the best for examining what he had found after he found it, and you know what a scholar he was in navigation and how long he was trained on the sea.

Providence seemed to order the wind and weather to be exactly right all the way for this first trip. If they had found such weather as they did on their return, we should not have heard of Columbus again after he left Palos, for the men never would have gone on and Columbus would never have given it up, so somebody would have gone to the bottom. Columbus' great thought had carried everything before it all the way up to the time he was off, and the weather

now, fortunately, helped to carry him over the last great thing. Much of Columbus'
The Journal of Columbus. own journal is yet preserved in what is called Las Casas' abridgment of it. This good man did not copy all of it for us for fear we would get tired of it, so he only picked out parts of it. The journal itself, sad to say, is lost. But there are some of Columbus' letters and papers yet in the world exactly as he left them.

Columbus had the worst men on his own
Bad Men on Board. vessel, where he could control them best. He had, also, most of the officers to help him control them. Martin Alonzo Pinzon on the "Pinta" had another lot, not so bad. The "Nina," the "little girl," was the best behaved vessel of the three, and never gave any trouble to anybody, and was the only one left to take Columbus home again when he was ready to start. In all my reading, I have formed a

great love for the brave "little girl" boat, for that is what the name "Nina" means. She was in command of Yanez Pinzon, who always behaved himself well, which is, no doubt, the reason why the "little girl" did the same.

Next morning they were out of sight of land, which was a dreadful experience for sailors in that day. Columbus steered straight for the Canaries. These islands were owned by the Spaniards, and no doubt they hoped to find a little of home again, for they expected to meet some Spaniards there. Saturday, Sunday, all went well, except that the men grumbled. Monday, the "Pinta" had a tossing about that broke her rudder nearly off. Columbus' boat came alongside to learn what was the matter, for he saw the boat was "rolling"; he found what it was, but he trusted Martin Alonzo to repair it when he said he thought he could manage to hold together until they should reach the islands. The next day something again gave way and it looked as if some men on the "Pinta" were trying to get it out of order so that she would have to turn back with them and take them home again. But Captain Pinzon fixed it up once more, yet in the night she sprang a leak, which detained them again, and after that they had to go very slowly; it was not until the next Sunday that they came in sight of the Canary Islands. The men had to stay on board and did not get back home again, after all. They were worse frightened than ever as they approached the islands, when they saw "a great flame" coming from the awful top of the Peak Teneriffe. It looked to them as if they had come to the islands that must be death's place, for most of them had never seen anything like that before. It appeared to be the very lightnings from God to punish this man for daring to go

Misfortunes of the Pinta.

out on such a risk. Columbus here hoped he could trade off the "Pinta" and get a better vessel, but he could not, so he had to contrive all sorts of ropes and stuff to mend it with, and it took him three weeks, but you see he did n't fail to do it. Pinzon and Columbus did not trust any one, but did it themselves. They were not ready to sail on until September 3 — just one month from the time they left Palos.

They had rather discouraging news as they sailed out from these islands about some suspicious vessels that lay ahead of them. Nobody knew exactly what they were. This was very strange, indeed, for it was the farthest out any one had ever been. Columbus and Pinzon felt quite sure they were Portuguese vessels ready to seize them, for Portugal claimed the right to discover just as much new land as Spain, and when one nation caught the other discovering the

The Pope Draws a Line through the Ocean.

same land there was trouble. The Pope finally had to divide the sea between these two nations. Columbus knew that, having been so detained, and the story of where he was going having been so widely talked about, it was very probable that the Portuguese were away out there waiting for him, so he sped as fast as possible around the place where ships had been seen. A calm, however, kept him back, but it kept his pursuers also, and they were finally seen no more.

On the 8th of September a fine breeze sprang up and sent them on down the world, so that the Peak of Teneriffe sank out of sight behind them, and it seemed to them that the last of land was seen forever.

A dreadful loneliness then crept over the sailors. A floating spar was seen away out in the sea. It looks somewhat like a dead body afloat, and sailors think it means disaster.

The Spar.

The pilots would steer the vessels toward the north, in spite of Columbus' commands. The awful stories of whirlpools, boiling water and dreadful places were always told of the south, so it is not surprising they preferred to steer away from that part of the world. But "due west from the Canaries until something is found," was Columbus' iron purpose and promise, and the men had to obey.

The Admiral's calculations had been that seven hundred and fifty leagues would bring him to the Island of Cipango, but he managed not to let the pilots nor any one know the exact distance they had come. His private reckoning was carefully guarded from anybody's intrusion. It was his own awful piece of business and nobody else had any right to know how far they had come.

Toscanelli's Map.

On and on they sailed. Then a most strange thing happened. The faithful compass seemed to be bewitched. They found

it wrong. They had sailed six hundred miles, and the bravest of them began to feel there was something the matter with the earth beneath them, for who had ever heard of the compass failing; and to fail them here, where nothing else could guide them, was awful indeed. Columbus'
The Variation of the Needle. learning and his imagination then came to his rescue, for he could guide by the stars, when they shone, and he also made up something about this variation of the needle by saying probably the North Star itself made a circle every twenty-four hours, and of course the needle would have to follow it. As they went on, the needle straightened itself toward the north again.

A terrible meteor shot through the sky one night and plunged into the
The Meteor. sea not far away from them.
This, indeed, they thought, was wrath from heaven. Ah! we may smile, but we must

remember what our better knowledge has cost somebody. We did not create it. It has come to us, else we would never have had it, so how can we boast of any superiority?

Between these alarming things that were happening, and while Columbus would be sitting high on the poop of his vessel, never sleeping, day or night, only when entirely overcome by weariness, two dear little birds came to them, which seemed almost like friends speaking. It was over the "little girl" boat that they flew. They were rock birds, they thought. Sea-weeds lay thick about them once, and it is a wonder they were not tangled up in them, for there is a mighty sea of them called Sargasso Sea. They thought the sea-weeds meant rocks, but they were very far from rocks.

They now had a fine, steady breeze at their backs which was, to their minds, a bad omen, for if the wind always blew steadily in this westward direction how could they go against it when they should want to return!

The men of the "Nina," again the lucky boat, saw some little tunny-fish, just such little fish as they had caught at home. This greatly encouraged them. Columbus himself began to feel that this might mean land somewhere near.

On the 18th of September, that bold boat, the "Pinta," which was so weak at first, took a sail ahead, contrary to Columbus' orders, and then the men dared to come back and tell Columbus that they had seen a whole flock of birds go over their heads.

Columbus had suggested to Isabella before he left, that ten thousand maravedis be offered to the one who first saw land, so, of course, each one was getting very anxious to win that; but Columbus really thought they must be only about halfway. The men were getting frightfully uneasy about the steady wind in one direction.

No more signs of land. The men were sure they ought to change their course. They thought they had passed some islands. Columbus prayed that the wind might change, and on the 22d of September, sure enough, a breeze sprang up, which proved to them they could sail home fast enough if it were necessary. So that trouble was ended.

"Never since the day when Moses brought the children of Israel out of Egypt were waves so welcome," wrote the brave leader in his journal.

On, on, they went, their supply of food getting lower, so that turning back might be a bad thing, even if the wind should force their commander to go back.

On the evening of the 25th of September, as the sun sank, there seemed to be a low, dark line at the edge of the water. No doubt men climbed to the tops of their masts and to those little "topcastles" I told you of, each evening. This night a shout came from Martin Pinzon, on the "Pinta," "Land! Land! Mine the reward!" All looked, and Columbus, even, finally concluded it was land, and said, "Yes, yours is the reward, but let us give thanks," and on all three vessels they gave thanks to God as the *Gloria in Excelsis* was chanted. The dark came on and they could see no more that night. It was, of course, an anxious night. In the morning how very sad it was to see no land at all. It had probably been only a low cloud.

IX.

After the terrible disappointment, despair took hold of many. Perhaps the Admiral's strength held out because he had to help the rest to live through it. Nothing so helps at times of great strain as to have to help others.

As dangers and fears arose, Columbus, the man, rose above them. Such strong character had in years past been woven into his life that nothing about him gave way now. His lofty faith in God, and in himself, and in his lifelong hope, now was put to its last great test, and the man and his God-given faith bore that test. Reason, also, bore him on. He remembered Juan Perez, Garcia Fernandez and Isabella—their prayers, their learning, their faith, all must have been turned over and over in his mind as he sat alone, night after night, watching the mighty, lonely deep.

But he was great enough for it all, because God was with him.

Four more days of the "everlasting monotony," and a frigate bird came to the "Santa Maria." Birds must have been as much to them then and there as Noah's doves were to him.

About the first of October, the pilot of the "Santa Maria" came to the Admiral and said he had gone as far as the Admiral had said he should have to go. He proposed to go no farther. The Admiral knew they had already gone one hundred leagues farther than the pilot knew, and it began to look to Columbus himself as if they might have passed the land. There had been no more signs of land for a few days, but, as usual, there came a flock of birds just in time to save their hopes.

On the evening of the 6th of October all

three Captains had a deep consultation. The Pinzons insisted that they should turn more to the south, for there the birds steered (they must have gotten over the fear of boiling places). "No," Columbus said, "we may miss all if we do." He kept straight ahead *west*. The next morning, October 7, early, the dear little "Nina" fired a gun. It meant land! The other boats crowded close up to her, but, sad to say, no land appeared. It was only low-lying morning mists.

Another consultation that evening. More birds had been seen going south. The Admiral finally decided to take more the direction of the birds. He remembered it was October, the time for chilly weather, but it was warm as summer with them. He knew the birds knew where summer always was, so the birds finally did the piloting (it would have been better if he had kept on west).

But the days again grew uninteresting. They could not bear it, when they had expected so soon to find trees and people again, and by the ninth or tenth of October things grew dangerous.

The men got together and made up their minds they would go no farther. Some have said they broke out in mutiny, but it seems they only summoned Columbus to come to them. He came; he appealed to them. Had they not seen signs of land? — had they not been kept from every disaster?— they had found no whirlpools, no monsters —many other manly words he had with them.

All that was in him came up to this sad last hour of trial, and he conquered the men. On the next day, the tenth, it grew to be very different.

It has been said that the Admiral promised that if, in three days more, they did not see land, he would turn back, but it is not likely. Columbus would have died first. There is no record that he said so, and it would have been more than foolish to do so then. On the 11th of October a higher sea came up than any they had experienced since they left the Canaries. Rough water seems to have been more endurable than the eternal calm.

Birds, still, but the sailors had ceased to notice them; they now had something more exciting. The "Pinta" picked up a real stick of wood. In the afternoon the "little girl" found a fresh bough from a tree.

As night came on the Admiral decided to head west again, and that they should "slow up," as usual, but both the "Pinta" and the "Nina" were too eager to go very slowly.

Columbus, in his high "castle" in the back of his "Santa Maria," took his seat as usual to watch, and about ten o'clock, ah! there shot across his vision *a light, a light,* from out the silent darkness.

He calmed himself enough to call one of

the officers to come to his side and to look also. Yes, he could surely see a light moving around, then it was gone again. They called the third man. He could n't see it. Nobody else saw it. Columbus was sure he saw it, yet it was dark as ever again, as on they went.

The "Pinta" was daring and selfish enough always to keep ahead of the "Santa Maria," which was a slower boat, and then Columbus' own pilot and men obeyed him better than the men on the "Pinta" did. Their orders were to *keep together*. But the "Pinta" slipped ahead, and at twelve o'clock when the watches all changed, Rodriguez Bernarjo took his turn in the "Pinta's" watch.

On, on, two hours more, and all at once, at two o'clock, as the moon broke through the clouds and threw a burst of light on everything—Ah! there before this man's eyes *was actual land*, only two and a half miles ahead.

What a wonder the "Pinta" had n't run herself on to it! if the moon had not shone out just then, she would surely have done so very soon.

But now all was delirious joy. Bang! bang! went the guns, and the other boats came up and all held very still until daylight should come, then there were thanks and prayers to God, and such tears of joy and gladness as this old Earth never before nor since has wept. It was the end of a mighty purpose conceived and borne in the heart of one great man. It was the end of a mighty pain which the Dark Ages had known for a thousand years. It was the beginning of a New World—a New Life. It was the birthday morning of our sweet land of Liberty—a new, sweet morning for the World. Is it any wonder we celebrate October, 1492, as we do this year, 1892? Four hundred years have been none too long a time for us to get ready to do it. One hundred years ago we could hardly have been ready, for we had only begun to have Presidents. It is only one hundred and sixteen years since the Declaration of Independence was written, but now we are indeed a mighty Nation, built by God to be very happy and to be very serviceable to all the world. So you see why we are celebrating this mighty birthday.

The Admiral now was worshiped by his men as truly as they had abused him. They had added much to his suffering, but that was all over now.

As daylight dawned and there in its beauty lay the land that seemed to have come out of the ocean, the men were all ready for work. Little boats were lowered. Columbus unpacked his best clothes and put them on, and the attorney for the King and Queen saw that all was done according to law, and we are told how very carefully Columbus came on to the land in the most stately fashion, with his banner and his sword, and took possession.

We are told, too, that he fell to the earth on his knees and kissed the ground.

But what or who it was they had found, they were several days finding out. This newborn baby was as much of a puzzle as many another baby is.

There were queer-looking people dodging in and out from behind the bushes. Instead of being dressed in cloth of gold, they had no clothes on at all. And they had colored skins and were entirely different from what Columbus or any one expected to find or had ever seen.

They ate no meat, they had no notion of fighting, they just seemed to be wild, happy, silly people, with a very queer language of their own.

Of course they were terribly awed at the great white men and their great ships that they thought had come from the sky. They supposed they were gods, and were delighted with them, as soon as they found it was safe to welcome them to their homes, and all were soon on very happy terms with each other, and with all the New World.

X.

It all seemed to be like paradise, this quiet, peaceful place, where there was nothing to fear, where there were no animals "except parrots." They staid in this place for two or three days.

Columbus now walked on territory which he was hereafter to govern according to his own will. The attorney who had come with him read to all the men the important papers which made Columbus a great man in their eyes. They had been given by the King and Queen to be read as soon as they should discover any land. A part of them reads as follows:

Important Papers.

"And we also command all captains, masters, mates, officers, seamen and seafaring men in general, our subjects and people who now are or ever shall be, and each and every one of them, that whenever the said islands and mainlands shall have been discovered and won by you in the Ocean Sea, and you, or whoever you appoint, shall have taken the oath and performed the ceremonies for such cases, they shall receive and obey you all your lifetime, and after you, your sons and successors from successor to successor forever and forever, as our Admiral of the Ocean Sea and Viceroy and Governor in said islands and mainlands, which you shall discover and acquire."

To the sailors this appeared to be very solemn power given forever to the man whom they had so mistrusted, and had thought so crazy. He seemed to them then to be a very different man, in his Viceroyalty, and all that. And it is a wonder that Columbus himself changed so little under all that came to him. His letters, however, read so simply and humbly that it is easy to be seen he was yet but a man intensely anxious to unravel a great mystery. His next terrible anxiety appears to be to have something to say that will please the King and Queen about the good they can do, and the gold they can have from this great thing that he has found.

He at once begins to discover the people. He has no name for them for he does not know what they are, but he writes about "these people of the Indies." He was sure he was at the India where Marco Polo had been. He writes in his journal on the first evening, after what must have been a very exciting day. He had not slept the night before; read what he writes on Friday, October 12th:

The People.

*"So that they might be friendlily inclined toward us and because I felt that they were

---

*Navarrete.

people who might deliver themselves the more readily to us, and who might be converted to our Holy Faith rather by gentleness and persuasion than by violence, I gave to several of them colored caps (or bonnets) and glass beads which they put around their necks, and many other things of little value, which gave them great pleasure and won for us their friendship to a marvelous degree.

"Afterwards they swam to the small boats in which we were and brought us some parrots, some cotton thread in balls, some javelins, and a great many other things, and exchanged them with us for other objects which we gave them, such as little glass beads and hawk-bells. In fine, they took all that we offered them and gave very willingly all that they had: but it seemed to me that they were quite a poor people in all respects. Men and women go as entirely naked as when they were born; of the men which I saw, there was not a single one who was more than thirty years old.

"They were very well formed, had beautiful bodies and pretty faces. Their hair was almost as coarse as horsehair, short, and coming down to the eyebrows [these were "bangs," I suppose]. They left hanging down behind a long lock which they never cut. Some of them paint themselves black; their natural color is that of the Canary Islanders; they are neither black nor white; but among them there are some who paint themselves white, others red, others whatever color they find. Some paint only the face—others, all the body; some the eyes, others only the nose. They carry no weapons and have no acquaintance with them, for I showed them some sabres, and as they took them by the edge they cut themselves out of ignorance.

"They have no iron; their javelins are sticks without points, some of which are finished off by a fish's tooth, and others by some hard substance or other.

"I saw some of them had scars on their bodies and I asked by signs what they were, and they made me understand that there came to their island troops of inhabitants of the neighboring islands who wanted to take them, and that they defended themselves. I believed, and I believe still, somebody comes here from the mainlands to take them and reduce them to slavery. They ought to be very good servants, of good disposition. I perceive that they promptly repeat all that is said to them, and I believe that they may become Christians without difficulty, as they seem to me to belong to no sect whatever. If it please our Lord, on my departure I will carry with me from here six of them to your Highnesses, so that they may learn to speak. I have seen in this island no species of animals whatever, unless it is some parrots."

Let us read on for a little while these very words of Columbus. They seem to tell us more than any others do:

"SATURDAY, Oct. 13th.

"Hardly had day dawned when we saw coming on to the beach a great many of these men, all young, as I have already said; all of good height. This is a race of men really very beautiful. Their hair is not curly but flowing; their foreheads and heads are very large, more so than any other race that I have ever seen. Their eyes are beautiful and not at all small; their color is not black but similar to that of the Canary Islanders and cannot be otherwise since their situation is with that of the Island of Iron, one of the Canaries on a direct line from East to West."

The reason why Columbus repeats this about their color being like that of the Canaries is, probably, so that he may in some way account for the color. He had slept over it and happened to think, maybe, that folks in the same line of latitude, had the same color. What color should he call them? It was a color no one had ever seen before. The Africans were black, the Cathay people, of course, were the Chinese, and were yellow, and Europeans were white, but what was the color of this new man? We have learned to call him the Red Man. How wonderful it is to realize that Columbus is the first white man who ever saw him and tried to name him and his color!

"I examined them attentively," Columbus says, "and tried to find out if there was any gold. I saw that some of them wore a little piece of it hanging from a hole which they made in their noses, and I succeeded by signs, in learning from them that by going around their island and sailing southward I would find a country, the king of which had large vases of gold in great quantity. I tried to persuade them to go into this country, but I soon understood they did not want to go, so I determined to wait until the next day in the afternoon, and then to depart to the southwest, where, according to the information given me, there existed land. The inhabitants of the country situated to the northwest often came to fight with them and then passed on toward the southwest to search for gold and precious stones."

The next day, then, we read of their exploits along the coast. Let Columbus himself tell of his as he approached another part of the island.

"As soon as day dawned I prepared to visit the different people, and before long I saw two or three of the inhabitants come to the beach, calling to us and giving thanks to God (as they understood some God lived up in heaven). One old man came even into my boat, and others called loudly to all men and women to '*Come and see the men who have come down from heaven. Bring them something to eat and drink.*'

"Then came a great many men and women all bringing something. They thanked God, throwing themselves on the earth, raised their hands to the sky, and then invited us to come to land."

He examined very closely all this island before leaving it, so as to decide where he should build a fortress; but he almost concluded it was unnecessary to build any place of defense, since these peaceful people knew so little of war. The King and Queen could decide for themselves, when they should see the seven natives he should take with him, "so as to teach them our language and to then bring them back into their country." "Still, if your Highnesses should command that I subdue them or take them captives, nothing would be easier, for with fifty men one could hold them all in perfect submission and do with them whatever one would like."

Poor Columbus! it is plain to be seen here, that his own wishes would be to act the missionary to these Indians; but he is also subject to a conquering King and Queen who have sent him to be viceroyal governor, and the question is which shall he be? He tries to be both governor and missionary.

Soon he sees so many islands he cannot decide which direction to take, but he goes to the largest one, "which is about five leagues from this one that I leave, and to which I have given the name San Salvador."

He takes with him the half-dozen natives, for he finally persuaded them to go, and moves on to another island, always going around their reefs and shoals in the most successful manner with his vessels. On the way to this larger island, a canoe of natives came toward them, alongside the "Nina." The first thing anybody knew, one of the half-dozen jumped from the ship into the canoe and away they went as fast as they could.

Columbus was anxious to have no trouble with these people for they had willingly come with him, yet if one escapes like that with a bad tale to tell it may make trouble, so they tried hard to catch him and bring him back and make it all understood, but the white men could not catch them. Columbus describes it in his journal and says they "ran like scared chickens" into the woods. The men, however, saw just then another boat load coming who had not seen the chase. Eagerly the white men held up balls of cotton to show that their commercial intentions were good. They would not come very close to the boat. The Admiral then ordered that they be taken by force, and so they were, but badly frightened.

But Columbus' plan was to take them and trim them all up with beads and trinkets, and give them presents, and then let them go again so that they could tell a happier tale than the man who had run away from them. Many little stratagems like this Columbus had to use to keep peace and to keep all under his eye.

It is very interesting to read about this cruising among the islands, but only a few of the most important matters can we here touch upon. The bits of dried leaves with which these men made a sort of stick and then set one end on fire and put the other end into their mouths and made a smoke, was a most curious proceeding, and one which our Columbus himself never took any "stock in," but the tobacco which these Indians smoked has been a source of much—shall we say wealth?

It remains, I think, for the economist of real value to decide about that. It has certainly been a source of much weakness to real manhood, and the world had been a much better world since, if it had not made this savage discovery of tobacco.

Columbus seems finally to have named these natives Indians. He is so sure he is in India that he falls into the habit, and he sets the habit for the world since. American Indians they are to-day.

These who were first discovered, who lived in such lazy, mild, happy ways, were very different from those found afterwards on the other islands and on our Continent.

XI.

Be sure to look at the map and see what a broken-up place our Columbus struck, and remember, what solid land—Florida—he would have found instead, if he had only kept straight west that time when the birds and the Pinzons decided him to turn southwest.

What a lot of distress it would have saved him if he had discovered the continent instead of these bewildering and numerous islands, these reefs and rocks and floundering seas. It was enough completely to break any man's heart never to be able to know what he had found. In all four of Columbus' voyages he went drifting around in this terrible hollow of wastes and islands which you know lies in between the two great Americas, the North and the South.

Bewildering Islands.

But God had a mighty purpose in this and Columbus was His own man. God's plan was that Protestantism and not Catholicism should have its chance in the New World. If Columbus, representing Catholic Spain, had struck the continent, we would all have been Catholics, if we had been at all; but as it is, England made us into Protestants, and Catholicism landed with our good Columbus farther South. Hence, Mexico, Central America and South America, and the West Indies, are Catholic to-day, while we are Protestant, because Spain followed up Columbus' discovery and planted her religion there. But we will not here and now, begin to get ourselves into trouble about the difference between Catholicism and Protestantism, but go on following the man Columbus. I believe it is Man, after all, Man with a capital M, who is going to save us, and of course

Catholicism and Protestantism.

you know I mean the Man Jesus, the Christ.

But let us get back again into Columbus' own boat and know only what he knew, and that is that God is good and takes care of every one of us in our own time if we will but do our whole part.

He wished to visit a small town because "the king who resides there wears a great deal of gold. I shall go to-morrow far enough ahead so that I shall certainly find the tribe. I shall see the king and shall speak to this sovereign who, according to the testimony of these Indians, has under his dominion all the neighboring islands, wears clothes and is entirely covered with gold.

"My intention is not to visit this country in much detail, because I should not succeed in fifty years, and I wish on the contrary as much as possible to see and to discover other new countries, and to return to you in the month of April, if it pleases our Lord. It is true that when I shall have found places where there are gold and spices in large quantities, I will stay there awhile until I have made as large provision of them as possible, and the only aim of my cruises is the search for these provisions."

Cruel disappointment is now beginning to weigh heavily on his heart. He remembers, no doubt, the great ado there was about the expenses, and he knows that there'll be something to pay in all his after life if this thing does not turn out well in riches. He must find gold.

As soon as the natives saw these white people, "they all took fright, abandoned their homes and their clothes, and all that they possessed. I would not allow anything to be taken from them, not even to the value of a pin," writes Columbus.

At last he succeeded in pacifying them and then they could not do enough for him. But he still wanted to find the king, and to go to another land which he believed to be Cipango; the Indians called it Cuba, but it was yet a long ways off. He sailed around among fruits and flowers, "but," he says, " my resolution is to go to the mainland, to the city of Quinsay, to deliver the letters of your Highnesses to the Great Khan, to secure his response and to return as soon as I may carry it."

When he held his devotions and talked with his men he must have more and more thought of those idols which the Quinsay people were worshiping, and of the good message he had for them of God and His love for everybody.

Searches for Cuba, the Golden Cipango.

He finally decided that there was no gold in sight and that he must move on; but he was troubled because many different winds were necessary for such roundabout ways as he had to take. He could go straight across an ocean with almost any wind, but you can see without steam it took very wise navigating to get around here among islands, rocks, reefs and shallow waters.

Slowly and carefully they felt their way through sands and rocks and torrents of rain for several days, and reached the beautiful land of Cuba. He had been told it had in it ten great rivers, and plenty of gold and had a great king. The beautiful harbor which, according to Navarrete, is now called Nipe Bay, is where Columbus landed, fully expecting to visit a real king. Columbus had never seen or heard of such ragged coasts, full of harbors, with mountains in the distance and great palms stretching themselves up like sentinels. Indeed, this was the land of Paradise!

Others besides Columbus have described the beauty that dwells there; but think what it was to Columbus, the first white man who ever saw it or heard of it.

Ferns and orchids, palm-trees, even fern-trees, all in tangled masses—fruits, such as lemons, bananas, grapes, all in tropical abundance—spices, then in Europe worth many dollars per pound—all seemed to him to be mighty riches; yet how in the world was he to make it into riches for their Majesties? No, he could only feast on it himself. Many times he wished he could stay there always. Yet he had a sad heart with him for he had two dear boys at home; he must not stay, but must go on.

Some of these mountains rise up four thousand and five thousand feet high, and away in there in the center must be where Kubla Khan was holding those great parties. Perhaps when the Indians said "Cuba" it sounded to Columbus something like "Kubla." Nobody knows. Anyway, where was he? He must find out. He did n't know. Nobody knew until years after.

As he brought his ships to land two little canoes came out, but ran away again. The Indians on board told him that there were mines of gold and pearls here. The Admiral thought the bivalve shells on the shore indicated that pearls were at hand. He named the deep, restful harbor, San Salvador. It yet bears that name.

Pinzon believed Cuba must be a city situated somewhere on the land where they were and that the land was not an island at all, but a continent whose king was at war with Kubla Khan. But Columbus determined to send in his letters to the king who, he believed, lived in this neighborhood in a city of Cathay.

He believed that he ought to make all efforts possible to find the Great Khan. One Indian finally came to shore and stayed long enough to let Columbus' Indians tell him that they were not subjects of the

The Very First Embassy.

Kubla Khan, and were not enemies, but were only good people who went around among the islands giving presents.

Columbus finally came to think this must be the mainland. If he was actually at the mainland then the Great Khan was in there somewhere, and he must get out those letters.

He had with him on board two men who were willing and well fitted to make the trip inland and carry the letters. Roderigo de Gerez was the name of one and Luis de Torrez was the other, a Jew. "He could speak Hebrew, Chaldean and even a little Arabic," and of course Spanish, perhaps French. He was the man to go and do the talking, for there was no telling how many languages he might find. Two Indians went with them. They took with them pearl necklaces and such things as would best pay their expenses. They were

The Next Embassy to the Khan.

to be gone not longer than six days. They were to bear the messages of the King and Queen of Spain, and to inquire as to the Khan's empire and strength, etc.

All this, sent in to a poor Indian! It is almost laughable now, of course, but we need not laugh.

The Admiral spent his time in climbing mountains and in hunting and shooting game. He shot some beautiful birds which he took home with him. He offered rewards for any one who would find the most spice, nutmegs or cinnamon, gum or any such things.

He found a fine beach where he had the "Santa Maria" and the "Nina" "careened," and "calked," so that they might all be ready for further work. You remember the "Pinta" was "fixed" at the Canary Islands.

The Admiral here heard of the great, universal, bugaboo story which it seems has been found everywhere in the world, the story of the one-eyed giants.

The One-Eyed Giants.

Homer, the great Greek poet, could n't have invented the one-eyed man, for we see the North American Indians had the same story. How does it happen? Can any one tell how it is that the Norsemen, the Arabians, the South Africans, the Greeks and our Indians were always scaring themselves about the one-eyed man?

The Indians said there were one-eyed giants to the southeast, and that they had immense ships and a great deal of merchandise, plenty of gold and pearls. This one eye was in the middle of the forehead, and some had heads like dogs. "When they caught any one they cut off his head and drank his blood."

These were exactly the stories Marco Polo

told, so Columbus was more and more sure every day that he was in India.

He found roots that when roasted tasted like chestnuts. These were our sweet potatoes. He also found coffee berries of a different species from ours. From this very spot is exported to-day more coffee than from any other market in the world.

He tried to wait patiently to hear from the men as to what they found. But all his hopes of Quinsay were dashed to the ground again, when on Tuesday, November 6, the men returned with no words of Quinsay. They could only tell of more Indians—but not a word of disappointment came from Columbus. No, indeed, he had to keep all that to himself, but we know he must have felt dreadfully lost after being so sure.

Return of the Embassy.

He very patiently heard their story and kindly entertained the new Indians who came with them, in the best manner possible.

The men reported that they had traveled twelve leagues. Then they found a village of fifty houses in which perhaps one thousand people lived. They had a fine time, however, for they had been entertained as if they had come down from the skies. The finest of the Indians had carried them in their arms to the best house—and had kissed their feet and made them sit on their best seats, and eat their best food. Seats they had not seen before in this new land, and they were only for chiefs to sit on; the Indians themselves sat on the ground all around them and looked at them while they sat down, and fairly worshiped them. The women, especially, thought they were very handsome, and all offered to go home with them.

"They begged the Christians to stay five days, at least. The men showed them their samples of cinnamon and pepper and other things which the Admiral had given them; the women explained to them by signs that there were great quantities of these things near there towards the southeast, but none in that immediate region."

They found very few cities, but at least five hundred people begged to leave everything and go with them to live in the sky. Is not that a yearning for immortal life? Poor things, even they did not seem to be contented to be only Indians. They wanted the next higher state of being if there was such a thing. But no, Torrez could only consent to take with him their chief and his son and a servant. He took these three and came back to the ships.

The Admiral talked with the chief and gave as fine a reception as he could, and would like to have taken him home to the King and Queen, but the chief was homesick to get back to the woods the very first night, and Columbus dryly says, "that as he had his ship standing on the earth," instead of heaven, "he did not know what whim might take possession of that Indian." As he did not want to provoke him, he let him go. He promised to return at dawn, but they never saw "that Indian" again.

We hear more about little sticks stuck into people's mouths, which are on fire at one end, also of sticks being held in their hands so as to raise a perfume. How queer! It seems to me the idea of carrying the tobacco around in hands instead of mouths is a pretty good one, for then it would not seem to be so ridiculous; but we have gone on with it in our mouths worse than ever the native Indians did.

They describe the cotton plant for the first time, just as it grows to-day. This makes four great discoveries in the New World; Indian corn, sweet potatoes, tobacco and cotton.

Columbus is greatly impressed with the native goodness of the Indians. "No malice have they," and, "I am convinced, most serene Princes, that from the moment that this devout, religious people hear their own language, they will become Christians."

Columbus did not know that quiet, ignorant heathenism was much more tranquil and easy than Christian civilization; but we would rather be Christians, and work and even fight and learn life and all that is in it, than to be heathen, would n't we?

I hope Christianity has done all its fighting, but let me tell you something; Christianity has not yet done all its discovering, there is a good deal of that left to be done by you and me.

XII.

Columbus still heard of the wonderful place called Bohio, or Barbeque, where the giants lived and had plenty of gold. With his ships all in good order he sailed on toward the "east-southeast," along the coast of Cuba. The same stories of Indians and birds and beautiful islands went on, but no great amount of gold was found.

On the 20th of November, toward evening, it was evident that something strange had come over the "Pinta" — Columbus noticed she seemed to go in the wrong direction. He hoisted his signals for her to follow him, as he was sure there was some mistake or misunderstanding, but the "Pinta" all at once seemed to have some notion or other not to follow, but to "run her own boat."

This distressed Columbus very much; he thought it possible the "Pinta" had diso-
Pinzon Is Gone. beyed for some good reason and would soon return, so he kept his signals out all night and waited, expecting to have the vessels all together in the morning. No, indeed, the "Pinta" was nowhere in sight when daylight came again, and, sad to say, she seemed to have really started for home. Could it be possible Alonzo Pinzon would undertake to run away in such a manner? If so, he evidently intended to reach Spain first and tell all the news, and lay claim to all the discovery. Yes, it seemed to be that way. Columbus had already mistrusted him since Pinzon had showed him "insolence" and disobedience many times.

Columbus quietly smothered all his pain and said little about this treatment, but went on bravely with his discovering, using the other two boats. He did not want to leave, for he believed if he could but sail on southeast along the coast of this Cuba— for he supposed to the day of his death that this was the mainland — he would surely find the Khan.

But he gave it up and sailed into the open waters again and came to Hayti—or San Domingo, as it is now called. This island is the Hispaniola we hear so much about in the life of Columbus, for it afterwards came to be a sort of home-spot for him.

Hispaniola.

He named it Hispaniola because its beauty was much like that of Spain. Hispaniola means Little Spain. There are some ruins to-day in the island Hayti of the buildings and forts of these early times.

About the first thing that happened at Hayti was the coming of a whole troop of Indians who were frightened at the sight of three white men, and ran away so fast that one little Indian woman could n't keep up, so the sailors took her with them to the ships. The poor thing was frightened nearly to death, crying, and supposing she would be killed when she was brought in.

But Columbus soon made her happy by giving her a lot of gay clothes to put on, and by having her introduced to the other Indian women on board. She was so happy she did n't want to go home again, but Columbus sent her there to tell the rest how anxious they were to make the acquaintance of all their people.

Sure enough, a whole lot of them came soon after, bowing and scraping and asking to be allowed to receive them to their houses, the woman and her husband at the head, doing the main business of exchanging courtesies. A fine young chief also came, carried on the shoulders of four other Indians.

No "Pinta" was seen yet, so it was pretty certain that the "Santa Maria" and the little girl boat, "Nina," were to do all the rest, and to find their way home alone when the right time came. Columbus had some hope, however, that Alonzo Pinzon was still hanging around Cuba looking for gold, since he was the one who was so very sure it was the mainland. It might be that he had not yet gone home and that he would still be found.

XIII.

When was there a time that Christmas had no place in our country; when there were no boys and girls who then had a happy time? Can it be that only Indians looked up at these skies—Indians who thought that days were all alike? They lived here for hundreds of years and never heard of Christmas nor of what made Christmas, until Columbus came. The world over on the Mediterranean Sea had, for all this time, kept Christmas as Christ's Birthday, but now this New World was to have a Christmas also for the very first time. Columbus had made preparations for it, and especially since he was invited by the grand chieftain, Guacanagari, to sail to his port and make him a visit.

Guacanagari.

This name is a very long one, but it will pay you to remember it, for he was the finest

Indian yet found anywhere by Columbus. His people were more civilized than others. When Columbus sent some of his men to visit him at his home and to take presents, they found real streets, that is, houses were arranged in some order, and instead of the people trading for everything, they desired to make gifts, not taking anything in return. They thought they were giving things to folks from heaven.

This acquaintance with the chief had been made a few days before Christmas; the men had returned to the vessels and all was well, more so than at any time since the little fleet had left home, except that the "Pinta" was missing. On the evening of the 24th of December, Christmas Eve, everything being so safe and calm, and Columbus very tired, having had no sleep the night before, and having been on watch since early dawn, he concluded he could have a night's sleep. He called the ship's master to take the tiller, as nobody else was allowed to touch it, and gave him orders to watch the weather and to call him if there were any changes in it. He then wrapped himself up for a sleep. The master then felt everything was so safe it was useless for him to stand by that rudder and do what any boy could do when he might just as well be asleep, too; so he allowed "a boy" to take his place. I imagine the boy thought he was the very one to do so and that he knew as much as was necessary, but little were his eyes and his ears trained to understand anything unusual. Little did any one know about the Gulf Stream and its currents. If "the boy" had been a young Columbus, he would have discovered they were drifting, drifting toward danger. How strange that Columbus, who had been safe in storms and among rocks, and perils of all sorts, was just now very unsafe, through this boy's drifting! When the awful sound of sand scraping the bottom of the boat was heard, it must have seemed as if it came right up out of the middle of the ocean.

Drifting wrecks are always such a surprise; all on board soon knew they were not in open sea; they knew what that sound meant,—they were stuck fast in the sand.

The Wreck.

Columbus was the first man on deck, and he commanded at once that the little boat be lowered and an anchor be dropped a ways back and an effort be made to draw the vessel off the sand. The men obeyed so far as to get into the little boat, but, dreadful to say, instead of helping to do anything they put off for the other boat, so as to make themselves safe, and left Columbus. He then, in his desperation, began to lighten the dear old "Santa Maria" by throwing all the heavy things overboard. He cut down the big masts, threw out the cannon, and did all that could be done, but it was of no use; it was dark and nobody could tell what was going on except that they knew they felt the vessel sinking more and more solidly into sand.

It was good punishment for the bad, foolish men who paddled off for the other boat, that the Captain of it would n't let them come aboard; instead of that he hurried straight to help Columbus, if possible, and let them take care of themselves the best they could. Nothing could be done but to get everything out of the "Santa Maria." She was fast going to pieces, for, with her hull fast in the sand and the waves of the shore twisting her every way, she was breaking up. Dear little "Nina" was the only boat left, and she had to carry one hundred men and get them all home again some way. It was a sorrowful Christmas morning for Columbus, but he kept up a very brave heart, and his very best friend was the Indian Chief, Guacanagari.

This was Christmas Day, 1492, the first one in America. It was spent not in festivities as it is now, nor as Columbus had planned, for he expected to have a fine dinner with the chief; but it was spent in saving what they could of the wreck.

The "Santa Maria" soon fell clear over on her side. Columbus and the men had to make their home on the "Nina." Diego de Arana, one of Columbus' officers and relatives who was uncle to little Fernando Columbus, and another man, started as soon as it was day to tell the King Guacanagari of the intended visit and of their troubles. He lived four or five miles inland from where the wrecked vessel lay. The kind king then did more than almost any civilized king could have done. He opened and emptied out many of his houses for them to come into. The people helped with all their might to bring everything ashore. In a little while the vessel was empty. Nothing at all was stolen or injured. Everything was honestly cared for, although there must have been tempting chances to steal pretty things. Who had ever taught these Indians to be honest?

King Guacanagari came the next day and made a call upon Columbus, and when he saw he was really troubled it moved him to tears. Think of such sympathy! He took dinner with Columbus and cheered him by telling him of plenty of gold that was to be found in the great mountains back of them. And he also invited Columbus to come to a fine dinner which he prepared for him out of conies (rabbits), fish, and roots (potatoes, probably), and fruits. Columbus found him to be a really kingly man, delicate in his habits and manly. When he ate (without knives and forks, of course) he always washed "his hands when he had finished, and rubbed them with sweet and odoriferous herbs." His people obeyed him and honored him, and all lived so happily that Columbus and his men began to conclude they were pretty good people to live with.

They finished the day with games and dances on the part of the Indians, and Columbus fired off some of his cannon, which sounded through the forests as if the heavens would come down. When King Guacanagari heard these guns, he was sure they had strange and wonderful guests. They exchanged a great many presents. Two large masks for the face, made of gold, were given to Columbus. The king laid his crown on Columbus' head and Columbus put his beads on the king's neck and all were happy.

After some days Columbus came to the conclusion that the best thing to do now was to build a little fort or house there, out of the wrecked vessel, and leave part of the men behind. He would then return to Spain and report all his news and come again as soon as possible to the men with new boats and provisions.

As they all became more acquainted, this plan worked well. The little fort called Navidavid (Town of Christmas) went up. There was plenty to eat and good water to drink. These Indians were the only ones Columbus had found who seemed to cultivate the ground and provide for themselves. The only trouble they had was from the neighboring islands. The Caribs lived on them and were much feared by these mild men, but the guns and weapons of warfare which Columbus' men had brought, seemed to be just what was necessary for the defense of this little New World, and so they made its first settlement of white people.

Navidavid, the First Settlement.

In the midst of all this confusion and what would have been distress to many another person, Columbus still found time carefully to write in his journal all that was necessary. He says, "I shall leave here a calker, a carpenter, a gunner and a cooper, and many of the other men who want to serve your Majesties and do me pleasure by finding out where the gold is gathered. And thus everything has turned out very conveniently for making this first settlement."

The Indians were delighted with the idea, and King Guacanagari did his best to tempt Columbus himself to stay, by chasing about for gold. He brought him quite a large amount; but no, Columbus must not stay. He must get ready to return to Spain as soon as possible. One morning, as King Guacanagari was taking breakfast with Columbus and deciding about two Indians who would return to Spain with him, word came to Columbus that a vessel had been seen.

Columbus knew it must be Pinzon's. He was glad and he was not glad, for you see since the "Santa Maria" was gone, Columbus was obliged to take up his headquarters on the "Nina." The captain of the "Nina" was a good man and, of course, gave up his ship to Columbus. But he was a brother of Alonzo Pinzon who had run away, and it might happen now, since Columbus was really shipwrecked, that they might together turn against him and keep him out of command. Columbus was, however, ready if things should take such a turn. But no "Pinta" came around, so things went on in preparation for departure.

Diego de Arana was to be in command of the fort. Pedro Gutierrez and Rodrigo de Escobedo were next in duty bound to keep perfect order and to "hold the fort" until Columbus should return. They kept the "Santa's" little boat for fishing and other things. They had seeds to sow in the spring and their main work was to hunt for gold. There were thirty-nine of them who remained behind, and all felt willing and able to care for themselves. They were Columbus' best men.

On the 4th of January, Columbus was finally off. Sad good-byes had been said. One brave little company was left in the midst of Indians, happy and brave, and the other was launching out into the mighty Atlantic in a small boat all alone. I am sorry to tell you they never saw each other again.

XIII.

Sailing away from the port of the "Town of Christmas" on this side of the Atlantic was a little different from the leave-taking of the port of Palos, on the other side, just four months before, was n't it?

These men had all learned wonderful things about a whole wide world in this short time. Geography would never again be the same. Columbus knew the secret of the ages had been unlocked, and that he held the key.

The great New World was now a fact. He had found it, that was sure,—but what if anything should happen to him and his little boat on the way home? He must have felt so small, as he realized all this, and feared that he never would get home with it; as if the waves and winds that lay between him and home would certainly try to tear it away from him. He seemed to be almost haunted with this fear. He knew well the mighty importance of his discovery, and that he was all alone with it. No one except two or three of his men cared for what was found. Columbus himself had studied the old Ptolemy and knew the world needed new geography, and he had gone out and made it all.

Alonzo Pinzon evidently knew it was a great find, but he had no such lofty conception as Columbus of how the very kingdoms of earth and heaven were to be changed. Columbus, of course, did not know about it all, but he came as near realizing it as any human being could. He was only human, and no doubt had many affections set on the earth, as is natural, but his treasures lay in the Kingdom of Heaven. He was discovering, living, dying for One he loved, and that One was his Father above, who blessed it all, and that is why it made such a great change in the world every way.

He bade good-bye to his New World and started toward the southeast along the coast of his Little Spain, not like some mighty monarch, but like a very tired man in a very little boat.

He had not sailed far when the "Pinta" was seen in the distance. Columbus tried to get near enough to communicate with Pinzon in order to know what might be the explanation of his conduct. Pinzon, also, made the effort to see him, but winds and waves were too high. Columbus retreated to a harbor near by, and it was good that Pinzon followed.

The "Pinta."

There they settled the matter wisely and carefully. Columbus said little. He knew the time for punishment or severe words was not at hand. He was rather helpless away from the help of all power of law and lawyers, but he knew, and Pinzon knew, that the time for his punishment would come when he reached Spain. Every obligation had been made very binding, by oaths and papers, and by signing of names, and all that. Perfect obedience to Columbus was to be carried out during all this trip, hence Pinzon must have felt rather badly all the way home.

On they sailed, after a few falsehoods had been told by Pinzon about losing his way on account of a storm. But some of the men on board of the "Pinta" told about gold the Indians had been bringing to them, and that Pinzon had been making plenty of bargains with them all, and had been simply cruising around. He had been rather lazy, however, for the boat had some wormholes in it which proved he had been standing still too much in the water. He gave up some of the gold to the treasurer on Columbus' boat, who had kept a very strict account of all the trading that had been done ever since they struck the islands.

Columbus describes something like mermaids, but he says they were not very beautiful. It is supposed he saw something like sea calves put their heads up out of the water, and as every sailor in those days had his eyes open for mermaids, Columbus thought this might be where they lived.

Mermaids.

Columbus still hoped those giants would be found as they left, and sure enough he did come to where men were fierce enough to cut their heads open, helmets and all, with one blow from their swords. They were painted and feathered in warlike fashion, and were strong and brave, and very different Indians from those at the little Christmas Fort.

The Eastern End of Hispaniola.

Several of Columbus' men finally took a little boat and ventured to shore to see if they could find gold. The great ships of merchandise and the one-eyed giants seemed to be missing. They found something new in the way of Indians and of Indian curiosities, but they found no gold. They succeeded in trading for a few bows and arrows, by being very careful not to offend.

Once the savage men laid down all their fighting instruments behind trees and came out very carefully to the white men to see them. All at once they grew suspicious of the strange white men and concluded they had better fight, and ran for their swords and bows and arrows and came on to the men in a frightful way, as if they were going to capture them, bind them and keep them as prisoners. The men had to defend themselves by shooting, and this soon sent the Indians flying for the woods, but two of them were killed; the men enjoyed that so much they would have gone after them, but for the command of the pilot on the little boat.

This was the first blood shed in the long, long struggle of years between the white man and the red man in our New World.

Columbus felt very sorry to have had this happen. It was new to have such bloody work going on. He was most thankful that Fort Navidivad was so far away, for these seemed to be very dangerous Indians.

Columbus writes in his journal of being disgusted with the company he was in, and of how he hopes to return to the islands with good men and vessels.

The "Nina" had come to be so shaky that Columbus could hardly take his observations of the stars or the sun. When the different pilots compared their calculations they did n't agree within a thousand miles.

Columbus' reckoning was different from them all, but his proved in the end to be right, but even he was not sure.

XIV.

Battling.

I am sorry to have to tell you of a fearful storm that came to the little boats in the very darkest midst of the great Atlantic Ocean. Others who have since been in these great storms in the winter time in great, safe boats, can appreciate what it must have been for little open ones that were too leaky and light to go through a peril of any kind. We know the end of the story and that they lived through, but try to place yourself with them, and imagine what it must have been to have seen those ugly, forked lightnings in the sky in the evening of the 12th of February! Real terror shot through all their hearts at once, for they knew they were in serious danger. Columbus had been all these five months on the water without any battle with a storm, and it had seemed as if God would not let any storm come near him; here was a fierce one, however, but his faith made a leap so high he felt sure that God would not let anything happen.

The morning of the thirteenth was a frightful one. Nothing but mountains of waves and a dark and dreadful sky, rain, thunder and lightning. Only once in a while did the two boats catch a sight of each other, and that was when they each happened to be on the top of a wave at the same time; then down they would pitch again out of sight. All sail was furled, and no attempt to move on could be made, only to keep right side up, if possible, and right end foremost.

All day and night of the thirteenth the winds beat on. In the morning of the fourteenth the "Pinta" was no more to be seen, and the "Nina" battled alone.

Columbus wrote, while in the midst of

these perils, words as calm and strong as if he were in some quiet home. Did you ever try to write when you were frightened or excited? I remember trying to write a letter during the Chicago fire, and I think there was very little sense in it.

Columbus Writes.

But below is a part of what he wrote while the boat seemed to be going to pieces under him. He had a little dry cabin in one end. Hear his brave words:

"Notwithstanding the quantity of water the ship is making [that is, water coming in] I have faith that our Lord who brought us here, will in his mercy and loving kindness watch over my return, for His Majesty well knows the toil I suffered before I could get away from Castile, and that no one was on my side except Him, only because He alone could read my heart."

People often have plenty of faith after danger is over, or plenty before danger comes on, but here is a man in the very jaws of death writing words of trust and peace. "*I have* faith that our Lord," etc., not that *I will have* or *had*, but in the midst of it all, he says, "I have."

In many places his writing shows how carefully he searched his heart to see what might be wrong inside him. He is evidently ashamed of being somewhat nervous and fretful, for Las Casas says that Columbus "confesses that even a gnat annoys him, and attributes such weaknesses to his small amount of faith and his lack of confidence in divine Providence, while on the other hand he is re-animated by the favor which he knows God has bestowed upon him."*

But the storm grew worse and worse. Hope was nearly gone. If there was any-

---

*Las Casas was the good missionary to the Indians, afterwards; he gives us Columbus' own words, sometimes, for he had his journal to copy from.

thing that could be done Columbus wanted to do it, or if there was any one of them who must perform some vow or become a pilgrim, it must be done.

We must remember that in those days men knew no better way to find God than to draw lots sometimes. If they only found Him, that is the main thing. You remember a woman once really found Christ's love by simply touching the hem of His garment. Las Casas says "Columbus commanded that they should draw lots for a pilgrimage to Santa Maria de Gaudalupe, when a candle weighing five pounds of wax should be taken her, and that all make a vow that he on whom the lot should fall should accomplish the pilgrimage. He commanded that as many smooth beans (or peas) be brought him as there were persons on the ship, to mark a cross on one of them with a knife, to then put them all into a bag and to stir them

The Beans.

up well. The Admiral was the first to put his hand in. He pulled out the smooth pea marked by a cross; it was upon the Admiral that the lot fell, and from that time he considered himself a pilgrim and as obliged to go and accomplish the vow which had just been made."

It was curious that Columbus himself should draw this, but he was as ready to make the pilgrimage as anybody, as soon as they should see Spain again.

Of course the one to whom such lots fell always felt as if he was somehow to blame for all the trouble.

It must have been a terrible trial to Columbus to draw this bean, but he did, and no doubt a most awful searching of his brave heart went on still deeper. Columbus was not so much afraid to die as he was anxious for his secret, that it be not lost. What a mighty desire he had to reach home with his news, no one can imagine.

The storm went on. All prayed and wept together. The little "Nina" mounted one wave after another only to pitch down again on the other side. Nobody could eat anything or sleep. In fact, they did n't have much on board to eat. Columbus was finally quite ill. His legs were so badly swollen from so much fatigue and from gout, that he had to stay in bed some of the time.

The next day they concluded to put the beans into the bag and draw lots again, and the one who should draw the bean with the cross on it should make a pilgrimage to Notre Dame de Loretto. This, Las Casas says, is "one of the estates of the Pope, a neighborhood where the Holy Virgin has done and does still a great many wonderful miracles." It was probably one of the greatest pilgrimages that could be performed.

Columbus did n't draw the lot this time,

but another poor man did. His name was Pedro de Villa. The Admiral helped him out by promising him to pay the expenses of this pious journey, for it was a long ways to go. The storm still went on.

Columbus retired at last to his cabin and did what no one on board knew anything about. How he ever had the strength to do it is a wonder. He took out his journal and made a copy of it, and carefully wrapped it up in oiled silk and then covered it with wax all water-tight, then put it in some sort of a small cask, and threw it into the waves, for he thought, and wrote down afterwards, that if all were to perish he would try to save the news of his discovery, and somewhere, sometime, some one might find it. Would n't you like to find that? No one ever has. He allowed his sailors to think he was performing some secret vow to God, when they saw him throw it overboard, for if the men had known how Columbus seemed to be preparing for death they would have lost all hope. He did n't let them know how heavy his own heart was.

Once more, for the third time, they put the beans into the bag and stirred them well and drew lots. *Again Columbus drew the marked bean.* This seemed so sad that for some reason they all vowed to make the pilgrimage together to the first church they should ever see. Columbus' keen mind jumped at a thought when the lot fell to him the second time, which seemed to have some comfort in it, and that was if he was twice chosen to make the pilgrimage, he surely was to be saved, and this may account for all choosing to make the pilgrimage with him and thus be saved, too.

XV.

Four days and three nights the danger lasted, but on the morning of the 15th the storm was over, the sky clear, and, best of all, land was in sight. God had heard and answered them. The great sea yet rolled and swelled, and still beat them about, but they could make a little headway.

Land and Clear Sky.

The morning was like a child's sweet face after a deep cry. Sobs and tears, waves and fog and chill, were not gone, but the terror and hurt had passed away. The sea always seems to sob after a storm like a heart that has been stirred up.

Columbus and the men all gave God the praise for their escape, and bustled about to get ready for the land they saw in the distance. Some said it was the Madeira Islands, some said it was the Azores, some that it was the coast of dear old Spain itself. Closer and closer they came alongside—to what? For three days, sometimes in thick fogs, they tried to find out. On Sunday the nineteenth they found a little harbor in which to cast anchor, but the cable broke and they had to go out to sea again in order to be safe. They could n't tell where they were until at last they sent a little boat over the waves to land.

The boat returned (with three men left behind) to tell them all that they were before St. Mary's Island, which is one of the Azores. Ah! the Azores islands belong to Portugal! In a moment Columbus was on his guard. He asked why those three men stayed on the land. The answer was that the governor of the island, Juan de Castenada, was so wonderfully interested in their marvelous story that he kept them as guests, and wanted to hear all the strange news they had to tell.

The Azores.

Oh, he seemed very kind. He sent out word for the commander to come to see him and tell him how it was they had lived through the dreadful storm. He sent them chickens to eat, and bread and fruit, and seemed very polite, indeed. How good the food must have tasted, for all on board had not tasted anything but bread and wine for a long time.

Columbus sent back thanks, but declined to make the visit to the governor of the island, though he remembered the vow they had all made.

He could see a chapel dedicated to the Virgin, not very far from the shore. It **Paying the Vow.** was not safe, he was sure, for them all to leave the vessel at one time, so they divided themselves into two parties. The first half of them were to go and make the pilgrimage and return, then the second half of them would go and do the same. Columbus himself stayed with the second half. The first party landed in a small boat, barefooted, and carefully and conscientiously carried out their vow. Columbus watched them disappear into the woods; waited and watched for them to return. Instead of seeing what he was looking for, he only saw, after awhile, a great excitement on the island. People were riding around on horses and with their swords in their hands; there seemed to be trouble.

Dear, good Columbus had no such reception as this in his Indies, where "no storms ever came." Here he was with half his men on the white man's land, facing something that looked more like war than anything he had seen before at all. He ordered every man to be ready for fight if it was necessary, but to keep hidden, for there was a boat-load, armed, coming to them with the governor, and Columbus did not want to show fight unless he must.

The governor came alongside of the "Nina" and asked boldly to see the ship's commander. I will not take time to tell you how the two commanders settled the trouble, but it was not until after a great deal of very wise and dignified dealing on the part of Columbus that all was quiet.

The Two Commanders Meet.

When the governor of the island found it was not safe to trifle with the Admiral of the Ocean Sea, who was in the royal service of the King and Queen of Spain, he soon "backed down," as boys say, and allowed Columbus and his men to do what was but right, and that was to refresh themselves and to perform their religious vows.

At first, you see, this governor supposed it was some crazy little boat-load of people who had been washed up on his shore. He supposed, also, that they were weak, and that they had been out discovering some of the islands or lands belonging to the Portuguese, and that his business was to seize them; but when he found out who it was, he was very much ashamed.

The weather was still so bad that Columbus had not much opportunity to mend his poor little boat, or mend himself, but he did the best he could for several days and then ventured on again into the deep sea waves, bound for Spain, on the 24th of February. For three days they went on comfortably, when another storm struck them which was worse than ever. They gave themselves up for the fourth time to the casting of lots, and, strange to say, Columbus again drew the marked bean.

The Weather.

It was midnight of Saturday, March 2, when this happened. Rain fell in torrents. Two long, terrible days of it and then, O, joy! land was again in sight!

Columbus now began to find himself in

the midst of business. He wrote a letter and sent it by a courier to the King and Queen of Spain. There were no postoffices and railroads, remember. Everything must be sent on horseback or mule-back, or by footmen. News spread from mouth to mouth as fast as ever news could, about the little weather-beaten boat coming into Portugal with most wonderful stories to tell about great discoveries. Columbus, who used to be hanging around the Court and begging somebody to help him do this very thing, had just been doing it all.

Two Kings.

He wrote another letter to another king, the King of Portugal, asking if he might come up to Lisbon and repair himself and his boat for the rest of his journey home. It was n't very safe to stay at the little town where he was, because great reports of gold and spices, jewels and such things, had brought crowds to see him.

The letter from the King of Portugal invited him to come to visit him at once.

A King's Invitation. He also ordered everybody to give Columbus every possible attention, and to treat him like a lord, free of all expense.

On the 8th of March he had a grand letter from the Queen of Spain, brought by a special person, Don somebody. This

The Queen's Letter. was the very beginning of honors which showered themselves on our Columbus for the next few months. Such awful ups and downs came to Columbus all his life that it makes a real fairy tale, does it not?

Here he was now, a wonderful man in the eyes of kings and queens and nobles, priests and bishops and archbishops, even up to cardinals and the Pope, but only a few days ago he was all alone in a little boat ready to be drowned and nobody ever to hear of him again. Yet Columbus himself stayed just the same, for he knew very well how his glory came. He knew his best friend, who went with him through his awful trials of waiting and poverty, and his perils, and had always known his heart, was the same One who had brought him his little human glory.

When Columbus and his pilot reached the palace of the King of Portugal, grand people came away out to meet them and they were escorted into the King's presence with all manner of pomp and ceremony and politeness.

Do you remember how he left Portugal only eight years before? Now the King makes a great ado about him. He invites Columbus *to sit down in his presence.* "What a wonderful thing!" everybody says. Who ever heard of anything so fine as to be asked to sit before a king?

Columbus did n't care very much about it all, but he sat down, of course. He was on the watch, for he knew Portugal would feel jealous.

Sure enough, the King, with all politeness, began to inquire about certain treaties between Spain and Portugal, and was very diligent in finding out exactly where Columbus had been.

Columbus very carefully told him just where it was. He had not been near the Portuguese lands, except to refresh himself, and his discoveries were away beyond anywhere that any man, so far as he knew, had ever been before. He told him how he had strictly obeyed the commands of Spain to keep clear of territory belonging to Portugal.

It is not surprising that wicked men counseled the King to try to keep all this glory for Portugal, if possible. They said if only Columbus would somehow sell out to them all his news, it would be a great thing. Columbus was as much a Portuguese as he was a Spaniard, and why need he take all his discoveries to Spain? It is also quite true that some wicked men proposed quietly to kill Columbus so as to prevent his ever being heard of again, or going to Spain; but the King himself did not listen to any such base proposals. He was too wise. He may not have been too good.

Wicked Men.

Every honor attended the hero back to his little boat. Cavaliers rode beside him and his pilot. Mules were presented to them to ride upon, and an offer was made to escort him all the way through the country to his home, instead of his again trusting himself to go around by the sea.

But Columbus preferred to take his little boat and arrive at the little town of Palos by himself, if possible. So on the 15th of March, just a month from the time he landed in the fog at St. Mary's, there he was at sunrise looking again at the dear old Andalusian coasts. The weather being fine, at noon he stepped his foot into the dear little home town of Palos.

There was no way for any one to know they were coming, so what a joy it must have been to surprise everybody. I wonder what the Indians thought of the white man's home?

XVI.

The bells were rung and the shops were shut, and the whole town of Palos joined in devout admiration of the Admiral and his men, and especially of the Indians. Friends and relatives crowded close to welcome them home.

It was Friday when they arrived, the same day of the week as that on which they sailed away a little more than eight months before. What wonderful changes! Juan Perez was there, ready to welcome his brave, true-hearted friend into the very holiest corner of his heart. How blessed it all seemed, to think that the man who came to him poor, so sadly alone in the world, had gone out and really done this thing.

And then we must remember they did not yet know how great a thing it was, as we now know it to be. It is easy to understand, I think, that it was God, sure enough, who pointed this man Columbus to accomplish a deed that will always mean so much to the world. He never did it as only a man. He lived and moved in God, and that is why he did God's work.

As soon as it was possible, the men all came together and finished their humble march, which had so failed at St. Mary's Island, to the first chapel they should see, for they remembered the peril they came through.

The Vow.

Others remembered it, too, for they had painful knowledge of how stormy the weather on the seas had been. Many had given them up as lost, and, sure enough, many were sadly missing. Where was the "Pinta"?

So it was a most solemn procession they made as they all marched in their bare feet and legs to the church of St. George. Great peace and joy and thanksgiving swelled glad hearts as the chants were given and masses said for those storm-tossed, weather-beaten seamen. But other hearts must have sunk down in great sorrow over the lost ones. Ah, how sweet it was to have actually lived through it all and triumphantly to give thanks!

Many, many things were to be attended to by Columbus besides his religious duties. Many accounts were to be settled, and reports to be put into perfect shape. The King and Queen were at Barcelona, quite a long ways from Palos.

What do you suppose then happened? There came sailing into the harbor another little storm-tossed boat, only a day or two after, and *it was the "Pinta."* What a surprise! The "Nina" supposed of course the "Pinta" had gone down in the storm, and of course the "Pinta" had thought the "Nina" was lost. What an excitement must have stirred the

More News.

little town! Here were all the Pinzon family supposing their proud Alonzo lost, but here he was returned to them; and others just as loving, were no doubt as happy as they.

The story of Pinzon's home-coming, however, is very sad indeed. During the awful storms, when the "Pinta" was missing, you remember, Columbus could n't think it possible she had slipped off again as she had before when cruising among the islands; so of course it was supposed the "Pinta" went down. Instead of that she was marvelously saved, and for some reason was blown off north, and came into the Bay of Biscay, touching Spain away on that side. This was Alonzo Pinzon's tempting chance to take all the glory of the discovery to himself. He believed Columbus and the "Nina" were in the bottom of the sea, and that no one would ever know how it was. He was

Alonzo Pinzon.

as nearly worn out as Columbus was, with all the exposure and excitement, but he arranged a report to suit himself and sent it to the King and Queen. He reported Columbus lost, and Columbus reported Pinzon lost.

These two different reports must have sounded very strangely. Pinzon's was received first, and the Queen was greatly grieved that Columbus was lost. O what glory Pinzon felt that he was about to receive! He thought of all he alone had to tell of the sufferings and heroic deeds he had passed through, and of the riches that were waiting for him. Columbus was at last out of his way.

Two Reports.

But what a mighty shock he felt when he came rounding the Andalusian hills, and saw ahead of him, all safely harbored at home, the little "Nina." In a moment all was lost to him. His heroic deeds were as rags. Nothing counted now, for he had an awful lie beneath it all. What a shame that he should have spoiled all his noble work that way, for he had been a great help to Columbus. Do you see how Columbus had just let God take care of Pinzon's wrong-doings, and sure enough, God did. Alonzo Pinzon betrayed himself. No one else did. And the Pinzon family, for twenty years after, brought lawsuits and troubles of all kinds for Columbus' descendants, in trying to defend this poor man, and trying to believe and to make everybody else believe that there was some truth in his claims against Columbus.

He never met Columbus again. When he saw the "Nina" all truthfully lying in the harbor of Palos ahead of him, he preferred not to be seen by any one, so he had the "Pinta" leave him a little below the harbor, nearer his home; he went there, and in a few days he died, rendering up a full and real report to God, who knew the truth all the time.

The "Pinta" with all the others on board came on up to Columbus, the real commander, and reported itself to him. He took charge of its accounts, and all its affairs and Indians, and was a desperately busy man, forgetting that he was worn out and sick, just home from a terrible journey. How sad that there seems to have been no one to welcome him to a nice home and to care for him personally! No one is homelike to him except Juan Perez, who entertains him at the dear old Convent when Columbus keeps still long enough.

The most important thing to be done, however, is to lay this whole affair before the Queen. She is the one most interested and most responsible. She is at Barcelona. How shall he reach her? By boat? No, the poor little boats are worn and almost useless. There are no railroad trains overland, but animal feet and human feet can get them all there, though it is a distance of about four hundred miles.

He received a grand reply from the King and Queen, who addressed him as "Don Christopher Columbus, Our Admiral of the Ocean Sea, and Viceroy and Governor of the islands discovered in the Indies." This is a long, great name, a very different one from Christoval Colon, and one that was a great deal more bother to him every way.

They promised him wonderful rewards and glory, and asked him to hasten his march to them. Their letter to Alonzo Pinzon was written about the same time, and it was crushing. He received it shortly before he died. How very different the two men must have felt, for one was guilty and the other was not. Columbus suffered, too, in after years, and did not receive all the rewards that were so freely promised him, but his sufferings were never to be compared with Pinzon's, for he never was false. He never betrayed a single trust. He was true to every one and everything. Pinzon died and others died all around Columbus, as false as falsehood itself, during the terrible tasks of finding our New World, but Columbus was sweetly kept from falling from the truth. He suffered, but not like Pinzon, ever.

He finally had his whole array of Indians and peacocks, the great snake-skins, canoes, arrows, spices, tobacco, India-rubber, potatoes, some gold, and the many, many things he had brought, with all the sailors, pilots and men, on the march to Barcelona.

The March.

The whole country was wild with excitement, and the people would hardly let them pass along, but in a month they all arrived at Barcelona. Columbus himself was on a horse at the rear, with Spanish soldiers to wait upon him and ride beside him.

The Reception.

The King and Queen made great preparations for this reception. They were seated on their thrones side by side, under a great, gorgeous canopy made of gold and silk, and placed in the public park where all the nobles could see the fine spectacle. Columbus entered the city as royally, and everything was prepared for as grand a reception as any king could expect. Columbus was almost dazzled with it all, but he did n't forget himself, and when he finally came before the King and the sweet Queen he so loved, he fell on his knees, expecting only to kiss their hands. Instead, what do you think? The whole of Spain was actually overcome with surprise. They took him by the hand and asked him to *stand before them*. More, *they stood up before him*. This was something so great to some people they could never get over it. They were bitterly jealous; yet through all the envy and the joy and triumph, Columbus was very sure of God, of Isabella and her friend, the first lady, and of Juan Perez, also the treasurer, Luis de Sant Angel, and Alonzo de Quintanillo.

The next few days were great days of thanksgiving. The royal pair themselves knelt and prayed immediately, before everybody, after they received Columbus, and from that on, the royal service of solemn music seemed to lift everybody "into heaven," says Las Casas.

<small>Thanksgiving.</small>

XVII.

I, for one, am very sorry we must come to our last words about this wonderful man, for there are three more voyages I might tell you about. But they would fill another book, and I can give you but a glimpse of the remaining days of Columbus' life.

He lived only ten or twelve years after the first great voyage. You remember he was nearly sixty years old when he made it.

"His strong youth wasted" before the "sealed gates" of opportunity; but in spite of his age, and wornout-ness, he still went on and made three more voyages. They were not so important as the first one, yet they were just as interesting, for they show us how a great nature can endure suffering and defeat, as well as success.

He never at any time lost faith in God, and he was always happy of heart, but he found out in a few years that there was nothing more for him to do but to go to heaven.

Queen Isabella and Ferdinand, you see, were made most glorious by this great discovery. Portugal was wild with envy over it all. She could hardly keep her ships and sailors from going to the Indies, also. It was like holding a lot of dogs by their chains, but they dared not let them loose. After that New World had been found, every country, as fast as it heard the story, wanted to have a chance there, but only Spain had it, the rest had lost it. Everybody wanted to go back with Columbus, and the Queen began to hurry him off in her first letter to

"*Christopher Columbus, the Admiral of the Ocean Sea, and Viceroy and Governor of the Islands discovered in the Indies.*"

Ferdinand was quite equal to all the great business there was in hand. The first thing he did after glorifying Columbus all he could, riding out with him, giving him a house of his own to live in,—he went straight to the Pope and secured his authority and power over "The Indies." Isabella had plenty of help in Ferdinand then, and some very careful statesmanship was required. He was equal to it, however, and watched everything and everybody and held on to all there was. He made it safe for Spain to go ahead and discover the rest of the world. He forgot, though, to keep all safe for Columbus in his old days, but he made it as glorious for himself as he could.

Columbus was invited to a great party once, by a grand Cardinal. Of course the Admiral sat in the best seat. The other guests were much distressed at all the honors coming to the man who once was nothing. They talked at the table very

One of Columbus' Puzzles

much as some people talk nowadays, about how, after all, they did n't believe it was anything very great to have made that discovery. But Columbus heard them talking, and his mind ran back to the long, long time when he wasted so many years; how he waited to control the selfish kings, how he suffered in managing those sailors on the way, how he so carefully sailed around among rocks and sands and among new people and strange waters; he thought of the perilous storm, but he knew it was no use to say anything to such men. He noticed a dish of eggs, and remembered an old puzzle; he was fond of jokes, you know. This one nobody knew about, he was sure, so he just took a round, beautiful egg in his hand and asked if any one could make it stand on end. They said, "Why, no, nobody can make an egg stand up." "Yes, it can be done," Columbus said. They asked him to do it, then; they would like to see him make an egg stand on end.

Columbus took it and gently tapped it on the table so that the shell broke just enough to make a flat little place, and there it stood, calmly as an egg could stand, right before them all. Well, it was a great joke. Nobody could say a word at first, then they said, "Why, that is easy. We could have done that." "Yes," Columbus said, "after somebody has told you how! It is just so with crossing the Ocean Sea. It is easy after some one has shown you how."

Ah, Columbus must have felt that his discovery of the Indies, like the discovery of making an egg stand on end, was no more his own. It was gone out of his hand forever. He was glad it was true that he had made the world so much larger, and he was humbly proud of the great blessing it would forever be, yet he very naturally did

COLUMBUS AND WHAT HE FOUND. 255

not want to be forgotten or neglected, or hated, after he had done so much, so he worked hard to do the best he could for everybody, supposing he would be taken care of.

By the 25th of September he was ready to sail again, with fifteen hundred men and seventeen vessels. Horses, mules, domestic animals of all sorts, seeds, grains of all kinds, were sent along, so that it was a kind of Noah's ark which sailed off from Cadiz for the Indies.

Second Voyage.

Fine, lazy men went along, expecting to pick up gold. They landed among the Caribbee Islands. The Caribs were not one-eyed or rich, after all. They were only wild, man-eating Indians. They went on to the island of King Guacanagari—called Hispaniola, by Columbus, you remember—expecting to delight the hearts of the thirty-nine men who had stayed behind to hold Fort Navidavid.

So they sailed up in front of the island, and fired guns for a nice surprise, but not an answer came back. Hearts sank as the truth revealed itself. Not a thing was left but ashes and bones. It was a sad shock to Columbus. He found the poor Indian king hidden away with a few of his men. The Caribs had been there, and the men had not always done right, so all was gone.

The Fort and Men All Gone.

Bravely Columbus rallied the spirits of all, kept friendship with the Indian king, and began to settle. But before winter was over so much sickness came to the men that Columbus had to send some of them home. They went and told dreadful stories of hardships, and, worst of all, they told false tales about Columbus.

New settlements were then made on the beautiful green island, one was called Isabella, the other Santo Domingo. It has lasted from that time to this. But matters grew worse, and in the spring Columbus had to go to Spain for new supplies. We are giving only glimpses, yet you can see from them, how the difficulties began to gather.

It was simply too great a discovery for any one generation to handle. It was two hundred years before it was possible for human nature to change even a little part of this great, wild land into anything like a country, so we need not be surprised that Columbus could not do it in a half dozen years. But he did all he could, and if those who were with him had but done the same there would have been much less trouble.

When Columbus went to Spain the second time he left his brother, Bartholomew Colombo, in charge of the Colony. He was almost as brave a man as our hero.

On his third voyage, made with six vessels, Columbus discovered the wonderful waters that seemed to come from the "Roof of the World." He went south of what is now called the Gulf of Mexico, to the mouth of the Orinoco. He discovered an island, which he named Trinidad, because it was to him like God, in his "Trinity," coming up out of the water in answer to prayer.

From this point he returned to Hispaniola and a new governor arrived at the island, Bobadilla by name. He had no business to do as he did and Queen Isabella did not intend he should, but he arrested Columbus and his brother, and put them into a dark prison for a few days, then put chains on Columbus and sent them both home. There were no questions, and no trial, nothing that could explain to Columbus what was going on, but there he was helpless with nearly all the men turned against him.

Bad Bobadilla.

The end of it was that Isabella was very sorry and tried to make it all right with

Columbus by apology, but Columbus' heart was broken. She also thought she could fix matters by appointing a new governor to go and bring Bobadilla home, and so he did, but Columbus' grand "governorship" as "Viceroy-General of the Indies," was gone. Even good Queen Isabella could not restore his rights to him.

This new governor was Orvando. He sailed for the Indies, and Columbus stayed at home this time. Spain was growing more and more glorious, Columbus less and less so. Though he was weak, he could not rest from doing something, so Isabella gave him four little ships, with which to make a fourth voyage. The first voyage, you know, was with three vessels, the second with seventeen, the third with six, the last was with only four, and they were very poor ones.

"This voyage was crowded with misfortunes, but more romantic than the boldest imagination would have ventured to put forth as fiction." Columbus was permitted to make it in the hope that he might find a strait, through which he could pass on to the real Land of Cathay. He was ordered not to stop at his own island, for the new governor would not care to see him.

Fourth and Last Voyage.

Fernando Columbus, fourteen years old, went with his father on this trip, and I am going to let him tell you something about it in his own words.* He says, "The Admiral in a small time had rigged and provided four ships, the biggest of seventy, the least of fifty Ton Burden, and one hundred and forty men and boys, *of which*

Fernando Columbus.

---

*He grew up to be a great scholar and wrote his father's life. We are indebted to Mr. James W. Ellsworth's valuable library of American literature, for the use of this rare old book.

number 1 was one." What a great journey for a boy of fourteen years to make! He saw some awful suffering before he was home again, but he tells it all in the most simple manner.

Columbus had to have a better vessel, and on this account and for refuge from a storm he saw coming, he stopped before his old place, "San Domingo," and asked if he might come into port. Fernando tells how it all was:

A Strange Happening.

"Thence we took the way for San Domingo, the Admiral having a mind to Exchange one of his Ships for another. It could carry no sail, but the side would lie almost under Water, which was a hindrance." How do you suppose a boy enjoyed the excitement of a vessel that would not stand up straight?

"So that the new governor might not be surprised at our unexpected arrival, the

Admiral sent Peter de Torreros, Captain of one of the Ships, to him, to signify what occasion he had to change that Ship; for which reason, as also because he apprehended a great Storm was coming, he desired to secure himself in that Port, advising him not to let the Fleet sail out of port for Eight days to come; for if he did it would be in great danger."

Now listen; this "Fleet," which was about to "sail" out of the Port for Spain, must have been an intensely interesting one to Columbus, for it was one of several vessels, containing much gold, his own among the rest, and it also was just taking Bobadilla to Spain so that he might give an account of his behavior to Columbus.

Here was this wise old sailor, Columbus, kindly advising them to wait eight days, for he believed a great storm was coming; and sure enough, such a storm came that

Columbus' enemies afterwards believed "He had raised that storm by Art Magick."

They all had great excitement and suffering every way. After the account of the storm, Fernando then tells us a fish story:

"While the Admiral gave his men a breathing spell after the Storm, it being one of the Diversions used at Sea to Fish, when there was nothing else to do, I will mention a Fish called Saivina, as big as half an ordinary Bell. This fish lying asleep above the Water was struck with a Harping-Iron from the Boat of the Ship and held so fast that it could not break loose, but being tied with a long Rope to the Boat drew it after it as swift as an Arrow, so that those aboard the Ship seeing the Boat scud about, and not knowing the occasion, were astonished it should do so without the help of the Oar till at last the Fish sunk, and being drawn to the Ship's side was there hauled up with the Tackle."

A Fish Story.

An interesting sight from the ship must have been this little boat-load of men flying like "an arrow" through the water, pulled by a fish! But the "harping-iron" had put a hole into him and the fish could n't keep up his chase for a very long time, so he sank helpless and they were then able to pull him up into the ship instead of the fish pulling them.

Fernando gives us a great many interesting and thrilling stories, one about an eclipse which occurred when for eight months they had been shipwrecked, and were sick, and many of the men had gone almost mad, some had died, others had run away to live with the Indians, and there was none to help but God. Columbus and his men were starving, but their lives were saved by a very ingenious thought that came to the Admiral.

The Eclipse Story.

Perhaps he had read of Tiberius, a great

Roman general, doing something of the same kind once upon a time, but this is what Fernando says of his father:

"He bethought himself that within 3 days there would be an eclipse of the Moon in the first part of the night, and then sends for an Indian of Hispaniola, who was with us, to call the principal Indians, saying he would talk with them about a matter of concern. He ordered the Interpreter to tell them; That we were Christians and Believed in God, who dwelt in heaven and took care of the Good and Punished the Wicked; that seeing how negligent they were in bringing Provisions for our Commodities, God had appointed to give them a token in the Heaven."

He then told them to look into heaven that night and see the moon grow bloody and then dark, and they would then see God would punish them if they did not do right. Sure enough, the moon grew bloody and dark—and the Indians took notice of it, and were so frightened they came running from all parts loaded with provisions, crying and lamenting, and prayed the Admiral by all means to intercede with God for them. So Columbus did intercede in good earnest for them to learn something from it all, for he was much interested in their being good. This was a curious way to save life, but "necessity is the mother of invention" and something had to be done.

Ferdinand gives us a most interesting collection of Indian stories of "Beliefs and Idolatry and how they serve their Gods," taken from a "manuscript of F. Roman concerning the Antiquities of the Indians, which he, as being skilled in their Tongue, has carefully gathered by Order of the Admiral." One interesting thing he says is, "They can neither read, nor count beyond Ten."

Columbus finally reached home again. He died two years after, believing, as others did, that he had discovered the East by going West.

He did not really ever come to want, for he always had friends and a pair of loving sons, who did what they could for him, and God made up to him in heaven all that belonged to him.

People did not make much ado about him when he died, they were too busy with his discovery. Only a few knew when it was that he went to his last home; but we in these days will never forget him. We shall always love him and help to honor him for his heroism and his faith in finding for the world something better than he knew, this Land of Liberty.